Rough Justice

A play

Terence Frisby

Samuel French — London
New York - Toronto - Hollywood

Please see page iv for further copyright information

ROUGH JUSTICE

First performed at the Apollo Theatre, London, on 5th May 1994 with the following cast:

Margaret Casely, QC	Diana Quick
PC Ramsden	Bill Champion
Judge	Alan Dobie
James Highwood	Martin Shaw
Dr Simon Kerr	Christopher Whittingham
Dr Hannah Radzinski	Jennifer Thorne
Jeremy Ackroyd	Jon Strickland
Jean Highwood	Sarah Berger

Directed by Robin Herford
Designed by Michael Holt
Lighting by Kevin Sleep

CHARACTERS

Margaret Casely, QC, prosecuting counsel
PC Ramsden, witness
Judge, High Court Judge
James Highwood, defendant
Dr Simon Kerr, pathologist
Dr Hannah Radzinski, paediatrician
Jeremy Ackroyd, solicitor
Jean Highwood, James's wife

The action takes place in number one court, Central Criminal Court, Old Bailey, London, and in the defendant's cell and a corridor outside the court

Time — the present, on two successive Mondays

**Other plays by Terence Frisby
published by Samuel French Ltd:**

There's a Girl in My Soup
The Bandwagon
Seaside Postcard (*One Act*)

ACT I

Number one court at the Central Criminal Court, Old Bailey

A trial is in progress. On stage are: the Judge, (High Court), Margaret Casely, QC, the prosecuting counsel, James Highwood, the defendant-in-person, Jeremy Ackroyd, the defendant's solicitor and PC Ramsden, a uniformed police constable. The "jury" is in the auditorium

The Judge is writing, Casely listens as she stands holding her papers, Highwood is in the dock and Ackroyd is seated, listening. Ramsden is in the witness-box. He is in the middle of giving evidence, using his notebook and facing the audience

Ramsden ... I was taken to casualty by a nurse ... There, in a cubicle, sat a man holding the dead body of a baby. The man had said the baby was his son and he had killed him ... The time was 11.40 p.m ... A doctor was with them. The doctor confirmed to me that the baby was a boy and had been dead for under an hour.

Casely My Lord, the court and the jury already have the written evidence of Doctor Bannerjee which confirms what the constable says. The defendant does not dispute this evidence in any particular.

The Judge looks at Highwood. Highwood glances at Ackroyd, who shakes his head

Highwood (*half-rising*) No. (*He sits*)
Judge Very well.
Casely Much obliged, my Lord. Yes, Constable.
Ramsden The doctor accompanied the man and me to the hospital canteen and the nurse took the body of the baby. When we had sat down I asked her what the ——
Casely (*surprised*) Just a moment, Constable. She took the body? And she came with you to the canteen? I don't ... surely.
Ramsden No, ma'am, the nurse took the body. He took it to the mortuary. The doctor came with us and she got us all a cup of tea.
Casely Oh. Oh, yes, of course.

The Judge looks up from his writing and regards Casely with a glimmer of amusement. Casely is annoyed

Ramsden Sorry if I wasn't clear, ma'am.
Casely That's all right, Constable. Continue.
Ramsden I asked her, the doctor, what the cause of death was. She said the man had told her he had killed his son by suffocating him with a pillow. The doctor found nothing to conflict with that. I arrested the man and cautioned him. He said, "Thank you, there's no need". He was most co-operative and was quite calm. I drove him back to the police station and turned him over to the custody sergeant. As I was doing this the man swallowed two tablets. We were concerned but he told us they were his wife's sleeping tablets. He gave us the bottle which still had some tablets in it. We tried to take a statement from him but he fell asleep almost at once. A statement was taken the next day.
Casely Thank you, Constable. Now then, this man, this self-confessed killer of his own baby son; can you ——

The Judge reacts

Is that not acceptable, my Lord?
Judge (*patiently*) Yes, Mrs Casely. You know it is. Just.
Casely Much obliged, my Lord. He gave his name as?
Ramsden James Highwood.
Casely Thank you, Constable. That's all, my Lord.

The Judge looks at Highwood

Highwood (*whispering to Ackroyd*) Is that me now?

Ackroyd nods

Now — um ... (*To the Judge*) May I, my Lord?
Judge Yes, Mr Highwood. It's your turn now.
Highwood Thank you, my — um. Um — Constable, I won't keep you a moment. Um — is — er — is this the first time you've ever given evidence in a court?
Ramsden (*surprised*) No, sir.
Highwood No, no, I mean, in a big case like this one —— (*catching himself*) I mean, in a murder trial?
Ramsden Yes, it is, as a matter of fact.
Highwood Yes. And — incidentally, you did it very well, very coolly. I agree with everything you said.

Ramsden Thank you.

Highwood Even though you got in a bit of a tangle.

Ramsden I'm sorry, sir I didn't mean ——

Highwood No, please, I'm not criticizing, you were excellent, I'm just saying that being here — in here — makes you very nervous. I know I am. (*He gives a brief laugh*) Huh — and not just for the obvious reason.

Ramsden Well, yes, I am a bit, sir. Inside. A lot, in fact.

Highwood That was my point. You said on that night I was calm. How d'you know I was?

Ramsden Well, you looked it. You behaved that way.

Highwood That's right. So now you say, I looked calm. If I were to say to you that I *seemed* calm rather than actually *was* calm, would you accept that?

Ramsden Yes.

Highwood Thank you. And your custody sergeant and Dr Bannerjee and that nurse would probably all agree with you, wouldn't they?

Casely rises

Ramsden (*embarrassed*) Well, um —(*he shrugs*) probably.

Highwood Yes. Thank you. That's all, I think. (*To Ackroyd*) Is it?

Ackroyd nods

Highwood Yes. (*He sits*)

Judge Yes, Mrs Casely, I know, but of course I intend to use my widest discretion. And I am sure that you, too, will exercise some restraint over any harmless errors he may make.

Casely ⎱ (*together*) ⎰ Most assuredly, my Lord. My point was ——
Highwood ⎰   ⎱ (*muttering to Ayckroyd*) Did I do something wrong? What shouldn't I have —— ?

Judge motions for Casely to sit and she does so

Judge Mr Highwood, just now you asked Constable Ramsden about other people's thoughts. That was inadmissible. But I do not believe you did it with intent, nor did you derive any advantage from it, so I let it pass.

Highwood Thank you, my Lord.

Judge As you are defending yourself, in person, it is my duty to assist you to conduct your case as best you can. Furthermore, as far as clarification of the law is concerned, you may be surprised and pleased to learn that it is Mrs Casely's duty to assist you, too.

Highwood looks at Casely sceptically as she nods, perhaps a tad sanctimoniously

Highwood I'm very grateful to Mrs Casely, I'm sure. *(He sits)*
Casely *(rising)* I fully concur, my Lord, that this was a relatively trivial action. But I wonder what it presages. The defendant is well used to public appearance and robust argument.
Judge *(drily)* Thank you, Mrs Casely. I think you can trust me to take care of you, too.
Casely *(equally drily)* You're too kind, my Lord.
Judge Thank you, Constable.

Ramsden exits

Judge *(to Casely, as Ramsden exits)* Yes?
Casely My next witness, my Lord, is the pathologist, Dr Kerr.
Judge This is your only other witness, I believe, Mrs Casely.
Casely That's right, my Lord.
Judge A remarkably simple case, it seems.
Casely That remains to be seen, my Lord.
Judge I expect it does.

Dr Kerr enters, goes to the witness-box and quietly swears himself in during the following. He has done all this many times before

Casely The defendant has pleaded guilty to manslaughter in admitting that he killed his baby son. I have only to establish that he did so with intent. That is then murder, to which he pleads not guilty.
Judge Thank you for the enlightenment, Mrs Casely. Most helpful.
Casely My Lord, what I meant was, *that* is where the complications will come.
Judge Yes, I expect they will.
Casely Now then, you are Dr Kerr; would you identify yourself, please.
Dr Kerr I am Dr Simon Kerr, FRCS, FRC Path, Home Office pathologist. I have performed autopsies for the Metropolitan Police for twelve years.
Casely And you performed the post-mortem on the nine-month-old Baby Highwood?
Dr Kerr I did.
Casely What was the cause of death?
Dr Kerr The child died from lack of oxygen to the brain, caused by suffocation, by blocking the mouth and nose. The means of blocking must have been some dry, soft object, like a small pillow. There was no bruising to the face or throat and no liquid in the lungs.

Casely We are told by the defendant, the father of the child, that he did it and that is precisely how he did it.

Dr Kerr Hm.

Casely And we have the pillow in question in court. It is exhibit one. (*She gets it from the exhibits table and holds it up*) Would you care to ...?

Casely proffers the pillow, but Kerr does not take it

Dr Kerr I have seen it, thank you. Yes, forensic tests show that it was certainly the child's pillow, and it is consistent that it could have been used.

Casely To suffocate this innocent, little baby?

Dr Kerr Hm.

Casely (*returning the pillow*) So. How long does it take to suffocate a nine-month-old, little baby in that manner, Dr Kerr?

Dr Kerr Well, say nearly three minutes ... to make sure.

Casely To make sure.

Dr Kerr Yes. You see, a baby would almost certainly be brain-dead sooner than an adult, but a baby's heart is so much more supple, it might keep beating for some while after brain-death. Babies are amazing things, they cling to life.

Casely And when the defendant did this to his infant son, how would he know when his baby was dead? I mean, without removing the pillow to look.

Dr Kerr Well, he could have checked his heart with one hand while holding down the pillow with the other, after the child was still.

Casely Still? You mean the baby would not have been still while he was being killed?

Dr Kerr Oh, no. He would kick and beat his arms about.

Casely How long for?

Dr Kerr Well ... say, well over a minute.

Casely Really?

Dr Kerr There would be a sort of crescendo before death and the limbs would still twitch and move about afterwards. I think there would be quite a violent spasm, even from so small a being, before it all died down.

Casely What sort of force would he have had to maintain during this three-minute suffocation period?

Dr Kerr Well, you'd need most of your weight — his weight.

Casely Without relaxing his efforts for the entire duration?

Dr Kerr That's right.

Casely Could such force have been applied accidentally?

Dr Kerr (*giving a little snort and shaking his head*) Well, no not unless ...

Casely Unless, what?

Dr Kerr Well, in some extraordinary circumstances of overcrowding or —
I mean, if you took the child to bed with you, or something, and rolled over
on him in your sleep, but ... not in this ——

Casely Not if the little babe were innocently asleep in his cot as was the case
here?

Dr Kerr No. It must have taken quite a sustained effort.

Casely Sustained for three minutes.

Dr Kerr Yes. It doesn't — um — I ... (*He shakes his head*)

Casely Thank you, Dr Kerr. (*She sits down*)

Judge Were you going to say something just then, Dr Kerr?

Dr Kerr Well.

Judge I am sure the jury would like to hear what it was. I certainly would.

Dr Kerr I was going to say, "It doesn't bear thinking about", my Lord ——

Judge Quite so. Mr Highwood, do you wish to ask Dr Kerr anything?

Highwood Yes. Please. Sorry.

Judge It is your right.

Highwood Doctor, you said my — you said he died from lack of oxygen to
the brain. Does that mean you examined his brain during your post-
mortem?

Dr Kerr Yes.

Highwood What can you tell us about it?

Dr Kerr Well, it's in my report and we all know, of course. The brain was
massively damaged.

Highwood You mean, *before* he was — smothered?

Dr Kerr Yes.

Highwood Can you tell us what sort of life the child had before him with that
sort of brain-damage?

Dr Kerr I'm not a specialist in ——

Highwood No, but you are a doctor, an expert. What would be your
prognosis?

Dr Kerr Severely limited in every way I can think of. No life at all really.
I'm sorry.

Highwood Thank you.

Casely (*standing up, quickly*) One question in re-examination, Dr Kerr. Was
the brain-damage to which you refer in any way life-threatening to the
child?

Dr Kerr No.

Casely Can you give any indication to the jury of the age to which the child
would have naturally lived?

Dr Kerr I don't think such a child would have lasted beyond forty.

Casely So he had thirty-odd years of life to look forward to.

Dr Kerr That child wasn't capable of looking forward to anything.

Casely Says the non-specialist. You know what cures, treatment, are in the offing, do you?

Dr Kerr I know of nothing that would have helped him.

Casely But then — excuse me — it's not your field, is it?

Dr Kerr No.

Casely Thank you. (*She sits*)

Judge Yes, thank you, Dr Kerr.

Dr Kerr exits

Casely My Lord, that concludes the case for the Crown.

Judge Thank you, Mrs Casely. Mr Highwood, you may now leave the dock in order to conduct your case.

Highwood Yes? Oh, yes. Hm.

He quickly goes to Ackroyd who whispers to him

Oh, yes. My Lord, we —I — I've only one other witness besides myself; she's waiting and I'd like to ask her to go first. My evidence might take some time and she has some very important things to do elsewhere — I mean, of course this is important but — anyway, her name is Dr Radzinski.

Judge Mrs Casely?

Casely No objection, my Lord.

Judge (*nodding at Highwood*) Very well.

Highwood Thank you, my Lord. Dr Radzinski, please.

Dr Hannah Radzinski enters. She is not foreign, and speaks cultured English. She carries a file. She quietly swears herself in during the following

Judge Excuse me for asking, Mr Highwood? I'm only trying to be helpful — but are you sure you don't wish to ask anyone else to give evidence for you?

Highwood Just Dr Radzinski and myself, my Lord.

Judge Very well. Thank you.

Highwood Dr Radzinski, would you please tell everyone all about — my son?

Dr Radzinski Certainly. Baby Highwood was brought to me ——

Judge Just a moment. Excuse me, doctor. One or two formalities. You *are* Dr Radzinski, are you?

Dr Radzinski Yes.

Judge Yes, of course. I have to make sure. And who are you? I mean — tell us, if you please, what your qualifications and functions are in this matter.

Dr Radzinski Certainly, my Lord. I am a consultant paediatrician. I qualified thirty-six years ago at University College Hospital. I hold chairs of one sort or another at teaching hospitals across the world. I have specialized for over twenty years in malfunction of the brain and nervous system, brain-damage in infants and many other forms of infant abnormalities. I have written four books on this subject. I no longer have my own practice but I act in a senior advisory capacity at Great Ormond Street, at the La Ligniere Institute in Geneva, the Peto Intezet in Budapest, the Goldbaum chain of clinics in the USA, the Instituto Nossa Senhora de Fatima in São Paulo. Oh, and one or two other places.

Judge Thank you, Dr Radzinski. And, should certain of your evidence be specialist medical evidence, I am sure that the jury would be as grateful as I, were you to use the colloquial, comprehensible terminology whenever you can.

Dr Radzinski I'll avoid the jargon, my Lord.

Judge Yes, Mr Highwood?

Highwood Hannah, Dr Radzinski, would you — um ... ?

Dr Radzinski (*opening her file, but not referring to it*) I first saw Baby Highwood two days after his birth. I saw at once that he was suffering from massive brain-damage. The symptoms were painfully obvious — classic, we inappropriately say. The post-mortem has confirmed that. This baby was a rare, unhappy, genetic aberration. There would have been no reason for Mrs Highwood to be screened during pregnancy for such a foetal abnormality: she had previously given birth to two healthy children by the same father, and, anyway, the damage would not necessarily have shown up. I examined the child whenever I was in London for the next eight months but there was nothing I could do. He was irretrievably damaged; there was no proper life in prospect for him. He would never speak or think as we understand it. He might walk — just — one day, after a fashion. He would see and hear imperfectly or, later, not at all. His carers would be lucky if he became continent by the time he was twenty. His physical growth-rate would be normal, reaching puberty, then maturity. He could well have survived into middle age.

There is a pause. Highwood stares at the floor before him

Judge Do you wish to ask Dr Radzinski anything else, Mr Highwood?

Highwood shakes his head

Mrs Casely?

Casely (*standing*) Dr Radzinski, am I right in suggesting to you that there have been remarkable advances in the treatment of brain damage since you qualified?

Dr Radzinski (*shaking her head wearily*) I'm afraid there was no hope of a miracle cure here. This was massive damage to the basic structure.

Casely Nevertheless, have there been remarkable advances ——?

Dr Radzinski Yes, in many directions ——

Casely — and will, no doubt, be many more.

Dr Radzinski No doubt. But we haven't moved an inch on the basic problem ... there is no way of making brain tissue regenerate itself.

Casely At the moment. Thank you very much. (*She sits*)

Judge Mr Highwood? Any questions in re-examination?

Highwood Er— no ... er.

He looks at Ackroyd who shakes his head

Judge Thank you, Dr Radzinski. You are released. This looks like the right moment to adjourn ——

Casely (*rising quickly*) My Lord, I beg your pardon.

Judge Yes?

Casely Forgive me, I have one more question for Dr Radzinski.

Judge Very well.

Casely Doctor, did anyone, anyone at all, ever ask you about the possibility of ending Baby Highwood's life in some way or another?

Dr Radzinski (*staring*) What do you mean?

Casely I'm sorry, I thought I had been quite clear. Did anyone ever ask you about the possibility of ending —— ?

Dr Radzinski No.

Casely Or of any various methods to do so?

Dr Radzinski Certainly not.

Casely Not the father, nor the mother?

Dr Radzinski No, never.

Casely Nobody at all?

Dr Radzinski No.

Casely (*ruminating*) Isn't that odd? Didn't even one single nurse or young doctor or someone ever raise the question as to whether a child like that should continue to live?

Dr Radzinski Now you've changed the question from the particular to the general.

Casely And did neither of the parents never even cry out against the injustice, the pointlessness, of it all? How they only wished it would all end.

Dr Radzinski Now you've changed your ground again.

Casely Nevertheless.

Radzinski (*firmly*) I don't think it my duty to disclose any cries of anguish patients may or may not utter while in my care.

Judge Thank you Dr Radzinski. Neither do I.

Casely Dr Radzinski, what are *your* views about the termination of such lives?

Judge Mrs Casely, you said one question.

Casely So I did, my Lord. Sorry.

Judge Are you taking the line that Dr Radzinski could be involved in the killing in some way?

Casely Certainly not, my Lord.

Judge Then let us allow her some other forum than this court should she wish to communicate her views to the world at large, shall we?

Casely Certainly, my Lord.

Judge Thank you again, Dr Radzinski. Members of the jury, you must not discuss these proceedings with anyone during the adjournment. Thank you. Five past two.

The Judge stands, bows briefly, and exits, as do Casely and Dr Radzinski

There is a crossfade to Highwood's "cell", represented by an area downstage

Highwood and Ackroyd walk downstage. Off, there is the enhanced sound of a heavy, metal door slamming and a bolt being shot. The two men move uneasily

Highwood Could that judge be on my side, do you think?

Ackroyd No, no, he's only thinking of the law. And he seems to be trying to — to keep the temperature down.

Highwood That helps me, doesn't it?

Ackroyd (*gently*) No, James. Sorry.

Highwood Maybe he thinks he can be easier on me if um ——

Ackroyd Life is mandatory for murder, James. All murders.

Pause

Highwood Yes. Of course.

Ackroyd Did you ever say anything like that to Dr Radzinski?

Highwood No.

Ackroyd And Jean?

Highwood I don't — think so.

There is a knock on the cell door

Ackroyd That'll be Jean. I'll leave you two. Just remember what ——

To Ackroyd's surprise Highwood is suddenly rather panicky

Highwood (*grabbing Ayckroyd's arm*) No, no, stay. I can't — I — *stay*.

Jean enters

(*Recovering himself*) Darling, hallo.
Jean Hallo.

They embrace, tentatively. There is an almost palpable constraint between them. Each of them may have much to say but cannot or dare not

Highwood How'd it look so far from the gallery?
Jean All right, I suppose. I don't know how it should look. All those hateful people in fancy dress just to ...

Pause. Jean glances from Highwood to Ackroyd

Ackroyd (*uncomfortably*) You got in all right, then?
Jean God, yes. Placards and demonstrators and ... I was bundled through the front door before you could ... They've made two sort of pens for the photographers.
Ackroyd Must've been awful for you.
Jean Well ...

Pause

Highwood Yes ... yes ... I'm sorr — I'm — how are the children?
Jean Fine. Thriving.
Highwood I mean Tommy — at school — and Alice's friends and — well — all this: their daddy on trial.
Jean Tommy's not at school. We're not at home.
Highwood (*shocked*) What?
Jean It's all right. We're together. In hiding, huh. Till you — till this is over. Tommy thinks it's exciting.
Highwood Was it that bad, then? At home?
Jean (*lightly*) Well. You know.
Highwood No, I *don't*. Tell me, please.

Jean Well, you couldn't get in and out of the house — the street, barely. You
had to run the gauntlet: photographers and — people shouting things ... I
got a bit frightened. Matthew's too small to — I had to have the phone
intercepted — and when some tabloid got into Alice's playgroup for a
photo I gave in. Sorry.

Highwood No, no.

Jean Anyway, I've done it now. I've run.

Highwood I'm sure you've made the right decision. You always do.

Jean Huh.

Highwood Where are you?

Jean A secret address, as they say.

Highwood Where?

Jean Secret.

Highwood This is *me*.

Jean (*hurt*) Oh, yes. No. I didn't mean ——

Highwood Never mind. Perhaps you're right. Even *I* shouldn't ——

Jean No, I meant, can anyone hear in — I'm sorry, Jeremy, I meant anyone
else — I — I'm getting paranoid.

Highwood No, no, you're not.

*They recover. Jean looks hard at Ackroyd, who grins back, clears his throat
and shuffles uncomfortably*

Jean All right, I'll be off. You must have tactics to — um ...

Pause

Highwood Um — yes, yes — I mean, give them my — um —

*Jean moves towards Highwood to embrace him, but cannot because he is
unable to make an approach. Jean suddenly clings to Ackroyd, to his surprise
and embarrassment*

Jean Oh, Jeremy, Jeremy.

There is a knock on the door

Ackroyd That'll be James's lunch. I'll — er ...

   He releases himself, and exits

There is a long, long, acutely uncomfortable pause

Ackroyd returns with a tray of food

Jean hurriedly exits

Ackroyd (*looking anxiously after Jean*) She — um — you and she — do you want me to go after her?

Highwood (*quickly*) No — (*recovering himself*) No ... she ... we haven't spoken, you know, not properly, to each other since I — did it. We've only seen each other with fifty other people in that dreary visitors' room at Brixton. This is not the moment for Jean and me to — (*firmly*) I can't open that can of worms now.

Ackroyd No, of course. This is all because of that fiasco at your bail hearing. I'm so sorry.

Highwood Wasn't your fault. It was that prick of a QC.

Ackroyd No, it was the magistrate. He lost his nerve. All those pro-lifers outside chanting "Keep our babies safe".

Highwood Well, perhaps this is cleaner. Part of my debt to ... it'll come off my sentence. I suppose.

Ackroyd Yes.

Ackroyd realizes what he has said as Highwood glances sharply at him. There is a moment of silence

Here. Eat your lunch. I wouldn't fancy the lovely Mrs Casely on an empty stomach.

Highwood Hah. Old Bailey grub looks better than the shit you get in Brixton. The lads told me it would be.

The Lights dim

Ackroyd removes the tray of food and goes back to his place. Highwood goes to the witness-box

The Judge and Casely enter and take their places as:

The Lights come up on the courtroom

(*As the Lights come up*) ... our third child was born fourteen months ago, a boy. We already had a son, now aged five, and a daughter, now three: Tommy and Alice. They are both normal, healthy and intelligent — (*he gives a faint smile*) up to a point. There was something very odd, uncoordinated, about our new son from the word go. Dr Radzinski's advice was sought. Within days she told us of her fears. Her opinion was

confirmed by her subsequent examinations: no hope for anything except
a twilight existence. He would always remain a non-sentient being and
physically incapable. He would, in common parlance, be a — vege ... a ve ...
(*almost inaudibly*) a vegetable. (*He can't go on for a moment and has to
breathe deeply to recover*) That is the first time I have been able to bring
myself to say it in public. It's — huh — almost a relief. I feel ... Jean and
I tried every avenue. We got second, third, fourth opinions. Our son's
condition was irreparable, inescapable. We searched wider; I went to
Switzerland, America. Jean went to Hungary. Even there, where they are
doing extraordinary work with brain-damaged children, no hope was
offered. There was none anywhere. Then Jean got pregnant again. Near-
panic gripped us. She and the foetus were scanned and tested as soon as
possible. The baby was healthy — especially his brain. Yes, it was a boy.
We had to make a decision: should we bring up both of them, or have our
hopeless, damaged baby cared for in a special place. I find it difficult, no
impossible, to tell you of my feelings as I went to institution after
institution, full of these — unfortunate children, or as I talked to their carers
and parents and families. And the older they got the worse they ... I saw
more uncontrollable, incontinent, impossi — most of them better, yes,
miles, *miles better* — with more hope — than our son. These places seemed
like a vision of ... I couldn't abandon our child to this — outer darkness. He
was — even though I sometimes — he was *our* child. I came home from
one of these trips ... deeply depressed. I stared at him asleep in his cot —
momentarily at peace — he looked perfectly healthy when he wasn't ...
(*He nearly breaks down*) I imagined him becoming the unspeakable thing
with no mind growing to maturity in the back bedroom ... I picked up the
pillow. I am not pleading, at the irrational extreme, the excuse of "dimin-
ished responsibility", or that "my balance of mind was disturbed". Nor am
I saying, at the other extreme, that I saw all ways were futile so therefore
made a conscious decision. All that happened was that ... that evening ...
I reached the end of that particular, dreadful road.

There is silence

Judge (*after some time*) Have you finished, Mr Highwood?

Highwood nods, head down

Mr Ackroyd, is there anything else you think Mr Highwood should bring
out?
Ackroyd (*rising*) May I, my Lord?

Judge nods

Mr Highwood, I wonder if you could help the jury a little more as to the effect that seeing hundreds of severely mentally handicapped children, day after day, in institution after institution, had on you?

Highwood does not respond

Judge I think we all got the picture, Mr Ackroyd.
Ackroyd I remember the wave of despair that gripped me when he first told me of — for example, my Lord — forgive my persistence in this matter — I wonder if I might ask you, Mr Highwood — James — what you told me of that institution you visited in the USA.

Highwood shakes his head a little

It was a place full of brain-damaged children whose condition was caused by their parents being drug addicts. You told me these children were known to the staff as "the crack kids". You told me how, as their parents seemed to feel no guilt, you took on all their guilt as you agonized as to whether perhaps, somehow, you were guilty of causing your son's condition.

Highwood is silent

It preyed on you. On your mind. Couldn't you describe that to us?

Highwood shakes his head

Judge I appreciate your efforts, Mr Ackroyd, but I watched the jury. Your client's method of telling his story seemed to have the desired result. I am sure we will have many emotional lilies gilded to full effect before we finish this matter. Does that conclude your examination?
Ackroyd Er — well, my Lord — um ...
Judge Thank you, Mr Ackroyd. Mrs Casely?

Ackroyd sits, frustrated. Casely stands. She is respectful and sympathetic

Casely Thank you, my Lord. Mr Highwood. You have told us a terrible story, a heart-breaking story, and as I said in my opening address any sane person anywhere, must offer you and your wife their deepest sympathy. For your wife to give birth in such circumstances is a misfortune which all women fear. And your subsequent efforts to search for every available chance for your little son, chasing every possibility, do you and your wife eternal credit.

Highwood But?

Casely No buts, Mr Highwood. I simply seek clarification. You came back from one of your many, admirable quests and one evening, looking at him asleep in his cot, something finally snapped, is that right? On the spur of the moment you killed him. Just like that. Simple. Unpremeditated.

Pause

I didn't quite hear. Did you answer me, Mr Highwood?

Highwood Did you ask me something?

Casely I was asking you to confirm your story of what happened.

Highwood You told my story then added your comments. From that I dissent.

Casely Which comments?

Highwood "Just like that. Simple. Unpremeditated".

Casely What's wrong with them?

Highwood (*firmly*) It could never be "just like that". It did not seem to me then to be "simple", though it does now. And "unpremeditated" means it had never crossed my mind before, which it certainly had.

Casely "It", in all that you just said, being the killing of your innocent, little, baby son.

Highwood You seem unable to utter the word "baby" without "innocent, little" tagged on to tug at our heart-strings.

Casely Don't you want our heart-strings tugged?

Judge Mrs Casely, shall we assume, in the interests of brevity and coolness, that all babies are both little and innocent until shown to be otherwise?

Casely Much obliged, my Lord. Mr Highwood, what of those parents — those loving, dedicated people — who have had disabled children and found in themselves unexpected reserves of patience, selflessness, love, in caring for their less-than-perfect sons and daughters?

Highwood What of them?

Casely Have you no comment for us on their characters?

Judge Mrs Casely, are Mr Highwood's comments about other people evidence?

Casely My Lord, the word "intent" is at the heart of the evidence.

Judge (*thinking*) Hm. Yes. Very well.

Casely So, Mr Highwood. What of those caring parents?

Highwood Admirable beyond words.

Casely (*gently*) Unlike you?

Silence

Some selfless people have even found joy in devoting themselves to disabled children.

Highwood I saw many such in the places I visited.

Casely It would be illuminating, would it not, if I had one of these people here to give evidence and contrast his or her actions to yours: a dedicated carer of brain-damaged children, not a parent, who would tell the jury of the fulfilment, the joy even, to be found in a lifetime devoted to those less fortunate than herself?

Highwood I wonder you don't rush from this court and take up a post at once, you paint it so invitingly.

Casely It's easy to be cynical, Mr Highwood.

Highwood Or to peddle sentimentality.

Casely It's sentimental to care for brain-damaged children?

Highwood Of course not, but I am not a professional carer any more than you are. I didn't kill just any disabled child, he was my son and he had no mind at all.

Casely At what IQ does murder become manslaughter in your view?

Highwood You know there's no answer to that.

Casely I'm just trying to understand. You have presented a clear, detailed picture of a loving father who has done everything possible for his afflicted son. The father finally snaps, kills his imperfect child and instantly throws himself on the law's mercy. "This wasn't murder, he had no mind. It was merely manslaughter, a technicality, please let me off". (*She pauses for effect*) Isn't that what we're being asked to accept, Mr Highwood?

Highwood I have simply told you what happened.

Casely You've left no vital gaps in the story?

Highwood I don't think so.

Casely Let's see. For instance, your state of mind. I don't think you've told us of that in full.

Highwood Huh. Enough was enough. You heard the Judge.

Casely I meant your state of mind *before* your son was born. Let's look at that, shall we? (*She holds up a sheaf of press clippings*) Now, you are a man whose state of mind is not unknown in this country.

Highwood I'm paid to express opinions.

Casely (*giving a warm smile*) Indeed you are. And very well paid by the look of it. You are nationally famous for your views on ... (*she flicks through the sheaf*) politics, morality, race ... politics, the arts, food even ... religion, ecology, politics ... sport, sex. And we also have the benefit of your opinions, personally delivered to us in our sitting-rooms, on the telly.

Highwood You don't really mean benefit, do you?

Casely You were even the presenter of a long-running, attention-grabbing programme which exposed so-called miscarriages of justice. What was the title?

Highwood *British Justice.*

Casely Yes, but wasn't it "British justice" with a question mark?

Highwood Yes.

Casely A huge question mark? Always printed much larger than the words "British justice"?

Highwood Yes.

Casely Thus bringing the concept into question.

Highwood The programme never questioned the concept of justice, whatever its nationality. It exposed the astonishing depth and breadth of incompetence, cover-up — even corruption — that permeates the British legal profession. We were knocked sideways by the public response and the — often tragic — stories we were sent. A national nerve was touched by that programme.

Casely In which *you*, Mr Highwood, were judge, advocate and jury.

Highwood The audience were judge and jury.

Judge Mrs Casely, do we really need to know the details of what Mr Highwood gets up to on television? He's a well-known media commentator on public affairs. Won't that do?

Casely Intent, my Lord, intent. I just want to be sure that the jury has his full state of mind in sharp focus.

Judge Very well.

Casely (*waving the sheaf*) Is all this just a question of an attitude for a fee? Come on, give us a thousand words knocking the right. Or the left. Or the centre.

Highwood I write what I think.

Casely I have here an article you wrote in one of our quality Sunday papers. It preaches the virtues of mercy-killing, as some people call it. It's most persuasively written. You have also argued for a change in the law in two TV discussion programmes.

Highwood More, I think. And on radio.

Casely And you took the law into your own hands, as far as your son was concerned. (*She pauses*) Well?

Highwood Well, what?

Casely I asked you a question.

Highwood I thought you made a statement.

Casely All the evidence points to a premeditated decision, a mercy-killing.

Highwood By "mercy-killing" I suppose you mean euthanasia.

Casely Ah, you prefer the euphemism; the euphonic, Greek-rooted evasion: euthanasia? It even sounds young and almost hopeful, doesn't it? What's wrong with the good, old Anglo-Saxon verb "to kill"?

Highwood has increasing difficulty in controlling himself during the following. Casely remains friendly, sympathetic and most polite

Highwood Nothing. I killed my son. That was private, painful and terrible. I have never advocated euthanasia — mercy-killing, as you call it, except in very carefully prescribed conditions, the principal one of which is that it must be at the rational request of the person who is to die.

Casely And when he can't ask you, and will never be able to, and yet is, in your view, clearly a person who would be better off at peace, then what do you do, Mr Highwood?

Highwood Nothing.

Casely That must have been agony: your own child; he can't beg you to help him out of his misery; would give you heartfelt thanks if he could, you, his responsible, loving father. It was your duty even ... to make the decision for him ... just a short step further.

Highwood (*crying out*) No — o. (*More quietly*) No. It's a long, long terrible journey.

Casely How do you know that?

Highwood is silent

You must have made that long, long journey to know it was terrible.

Highwood Some of it but I — always drew back. What happened was not that.

Casely So you considered killing him?

Highwood We considered *everything*.

Casely Or should I say euthanasing him? What is the gloss-word you people use? Putting him to sleep? Like a vet with a pet dog?

Highwood Which particular barrel did you scrape for that one?

Casely A very distinguished barrel: Thursday's edition of *The Telegraph*. But I could have had my pick, there is a nation-wide furore over this case. All we hear is "you should have" or "you shouldn't have" killed the babe. The media are having a field day. Your story will be worth many thousands and you know it and cannot escape it.

Highwood (*shocked*) I wouldn't dream of taking money because of ——

Casely never lets up for a second on her kind, thoughtful manner as she puts the boot in, accelerating Highwood's rise in temperature

Casely   }   { Be careful, Mr Highwood.
Highwood } (*together*) { How dare you? What are you suggesting?

Casely You are under oath. Don't dig a hole for yourself that you may bitterly regret.

Highwood No. Never.

Casely Will you never utter in public on the subject again?

Highwood Of course I will, but any income we derived we'd give away, donate to charity, make sure that ——

Casely Ssh. Please. Don't excite yourself. I am sure you mean what you say. Now. But life has a funny way of turning such promises into unbearable millstones ——

Highwood How dare you? This is preposterous. How can you suggest —— ?

Casely Well, let's look at the worst-case scenario — from your point of view, of course. Suppose you are put in jail. Who will pay the bills? Your wife has merely a fraction of your earning power. But, wait. She has only to speak out about her experiences in this killing and up rockets her value to the media. Do you still think you'd both be strong enough to resist the temptation?

Highwood Yes.

Casely With your living children in real need?

Highwood I've said, yes.

But it looks thin

Casely Anything could happen: accident, divorce, your death even.

Highwood (*stubbornly*) I can imagine no circumstances in which Jean or I would capitalize on our son's death.

Casely I am sure the jury have more effective imaginations.

Highwood (*bitterly*) Are you trying to pretend I did this for profit?

Casely (*warmly*) Of course I'm not, Mr Highwood. And you know it. I am visualizing the real world. You cannot stop yourself earning thousands from this trial and we both knew it all along yet you *will not admit it* to us. Nor to yourself, perhaps. What else are you not admitting? (*She lets that hang for a moment*) Let's have a closer look at your beliefs on mercy-killing.

Highwood My Lord, surely none of this is relevant or permissible or whatever you call it. First her smear about money, now this.

Judge It all seems relevant to me, Mr Highwood.

Casely So you believe in, and have publicly advocated mercy-killing?

Highwood (*goaded too far*) If you're going to trail red herrings in this way, I think I should do the same. You are a well-known devout Roman Catholic. You are a public supporter of the Anti-Abortion League, the Pro-Life Association and the anti-contraception brigade ——

Casely	} (*together*) {	I fail to see how ——
Judge		Mr Highwood ——

Highwood — even suicide is still a mortal sin to you though it is no longer against the law in this country. You want to turn this trial into a public debate on the right of a person to end his own life ——
Judge Mr Highwood ——
Highwood — when it is really a horribly private matter.
Judge *Mr Highwood.*
Highwood And it looks as though there was some very funny skulduggery somewhere in *your* being appointed to prosecute and persecute ——
Judge *Silence.*
Highwood — in this way: a prominent QC who's a married woman and mother. That's a pretty rare bird.
Judge The private views of a professional advocate are not ——
Highwood I don't see why her views are less relevant than mine.
Judge You are deliberately attempting to subvert the process of this trial and you know it.
Highwood Or possibly yours for that matter. You're in the perfect position to manipulate the jury.
Judge (*furiously*) I was about to say that what you said earlier could have been construed as contempt, but that last remark certainly was.
Highwood Is it contempt to state what is a self-evident truth? That should enhance your authority if it's ——
Judge Silence, silence ——
Highwood — soundly based. All right, I've finished, my Lord. Thank you.

There is a moment as the Judge gathers himself

Judge Members of the jury, you will ignore that last exchange. Mrs Casely's private views are not relevant. Nor are mine. Now I must ask you to retire while I consider a matter of law in your absence. I remind you that you may not discuss these proceedings with anyone. Thank you.

He takes a moment for the jury to leave

Now, Mrs Casely, should this hearing be aborted and a new jury sworn in? Have you any thoughts to offer me on that subject?
Casely My Lord, you could be doing exactly what he wanted when he staged his outburst.
Judge The same thought had occurred to me.
Casely We could have scene after scene while he rid himself of a jury, you, me, or any other advocate he didn't care for.
Judge Thank you. Take him down. The court is adjourned for thirty minutes.

He rises, bows and exits. The rest of the court follow suit

Highwood and Ackroyd move downstage and the Lights change. We once again hear the sound of a cell-door slamming off stage. Ackroyd is not pleased but tries to put a face on it. Highwood is very upset. They are not a reassuring sight

Highwood I'm sorry, Jeremy, but it was the "making money out of it" bit that got me going.

Ackroyd That's what she was trying to do. Now you don't only face life for murder you could be doing extra time for contempt.

Highwood That judge won't do anything on that ... will he?

Ackroyd Who knows? If the jury find you not guilty of murder, the Judge still has discretion to give you anything up to life on the manslaughter charge. For goodness sake *don't upset him again.*

Highwood We agreed I would drag Casely into the open at some point.

Ackroyd But not like that.

Highwood Will he order a re-trial?

Ackroyd shrugs

He'll keep the case, it'll make him famous.

Ackroyd Such factors do not enter a judge's deliberations.

Highwood Huh.

Ackroyd We don't know enough about him, do we? He's never said, "Who are the Beatles?" and he's never shown up anywhere on the side of liberal issues. All I found in *Who's Who* was that he's C of E, so at least he's not burdened with religious dogma.

There is a knock on the door

Highwood (*urgently*) That'll be Jean. Same thing goes, Jeremy. Don't leave us alone.

Ackroyd (*unhappily*) You have to face her sometime, you know.

Highwood just shakes his head, hopelessly lost

Jean enters

Highwood (*presenting a good face*) How did it look from the public gallery?

Jean Well, of course, the Judge was steaming. Casely just looked satisfied.

Ackroyd That's her professional face. She looks like that even when she knows she's losing.

Jean God, I loathe that woman.

Ackroyd Don't even begin to think about her like that, James. Remember your objective. She's fifty times more subtle that she looks.

Highwood Trained by Jesuits, I'm sure.

Jean The jury don't seem to react at all. Some of them look directly at me, others won't. One woman cried when you talked about ...

Highwood Jeremy thinks everything went wrong immediately after that.

Jean (*to Jeremy*) Hm?

Ackroyd Well ... Casely's making progress, isn't she? Trying to make James look — well ——

Highwood Dishonest.

Ackroyd Not exactly dishonest ——

Jean Oh, no. You don't come across like that at all.

Ackroyd Jean — well — not everyone has your view of James. I mean — well — look at it from the jury's point of view. James's got everything: money, glamorous job, fame, they even look up into the gallery and see you. Casely's trying to reduce James from a popular, famous object of sympathy to being a bit — well — shifty, whereas James has got to be — *loved* by them, I suppose. The trouble is he's almost too clever for them to feel sorry for him. You see, James, it's what I feared: you can't be both victim and victor in this trial. I say again. It's not too late to get a QC, a top man who'll ——

Highwood No.

Ackroyd — give you space to play the sympathetic role and who'll put the boot in, like Casely, when it comes to arguing *for* you ——

Highwood Like that barrister did at my bail proceedings ——

Ackroyd — that was unfortunate, James; an aberration ——

Highwood — six months ago.

Ackroyd — it was the *magistrate's* fault.

Highwood What does it matter which of them it was? If I'm going to spend years inside ——

Jean Don't, Jimmy, please ——

Highwood — it'll be because *I* failed not because I watched some insincere prick of a lawyer screw it up for me.

Ackroyd I think that TV programme of yours has clouded your judgement ——

Highwood Oh, I don't mean you, Jeremy. I don't even think of you as a lawyer ——

Ackroyd You could have re-applied, James. I'm sure you'd've won.

Highwood You were sure I'd win the first hearing.

Jean Yes, why didn't you re-apply, Jimmy?

Silence for a moment. He can't answer

(*Knowing*) Yes.

Ackroyd Every person who ever lost a legal battle shouts "foul", and there's always one loser from every court case ——
Highwood But there are always at *least* two winners ——
Jean Stop it, you two.
Highwood — the lawyers.
Ackroyd All right, OK. I give in. Just beware of that judge.
Highwood I am. He frightens the life out of me.
Ackroyd Well, *show* it. Get some sympathy.
Highwood Ha. I thought I *was* showing it. My God, I'm feeling it. I'm shitting bricks every minute I'm out there.
Jean In that case, Jimmy, why don't you let Jeremy talk to —— ?
Highwood (*raging*) No, *no*, NO.

Jean is shocked into silence by this outburst

(*Instantly contrite*) I'm sorry, darling, I didn't mean to — listen — (*he holds her*) we cannot change horses in midstream just because I'm frightened. I can live with failing at what I'm doing. I couldn't face any other — well.

After a moment she breaks away from him

Silence

Ackroyd (*going*) I'll just ——
Jean It's all right, Jeremy. Don't go.
Ackroyd I'll be just outside if you ——
Jean *No*. Don't leave us. We neither of us dare.
Ackroyd Oh.
Jean I think Jeremy's wrong.
Highwood What?
Jean (*looking in her handbag*) About the emotion. Every time you let go the atmosphere in there is electric. Unbearable almost. But when you went for — I mean, argued with the Judge: was that wise?
Highwood I was trying to separate the jury from the Judge without antagonizing the Judge. I failed.
Jean I've brought you these. From the children.
Highwood Oh.

Jean hands some children's drawings to Highwood

This is terrific. Alice really can draw, can't she?

Jean She drives me mad: one eye in a book and the other on the telly, she dashes something off then shoves it aside.

Highwood It's called talent.

Jean Something that Tommy clearly doesn't have.

Highwood gives snort of amusement at Tommy's effort; it is almost a sob

Highwood I love it.

Jean (*handing him the last one*) I put Matthew's hands in the paint and let him slap them on the paper for you. There. From him.

Highwood (*choked with emotion; he can hardly speak*) Oh, it's wonderful. Little hands ...

Jean (*to Jeremy*) Jimmy's never seen him, you know: Matthew.

Ackroyd What?

Jean When I took him to Brixton, visiting, they wouldn't let me — some official, some officer somewhere said that as James was a confessed child-killer it wouldn't be safe to ——

Ackroyd Why ever didn't you tell me? I would have ——

Jean So perhaps he's right. There's always one somewhere, some anonymous official ... who'll screw it all ...

Silence

Highwood (*showing the paper to Ackroyd*) He's left-handed.

The Lights change; the whole courtroom is seen

Judge and Casely enter

Jean exits

Highwood returns to the dock and Ackroyd goes to his place

Judge Highwood, stand up.

Highwood stands

I have considered the matter of a possible contempt of court. I always try to allow a defendant-in-person the maximum lenience, but you were searching, I feel sure, for any chance to expose the private views of Mrs Casely to the jury in order improperly to aid your cause. That is a contempt of court and I think you knew it. I shall deal with that after the trial of the main matter is finished. As for that staged display of apparently sincere indignation, I shall look with great scepticism on any further emotional outbursts from you. I shall continue to hear the main trial, and with this jury. I shall not allow you to impose your will on the due and proper processes of law. Recall the jury. You may return to the witness-box.

Highwood does so

Ladies and gentlemen of the jury, your duty is to ignore completely the outburst by the defendant. This is a very difficult matter for him and you must make every allowance. Yes, Mrs Casely.

Casely stands

Highwood (*simultaneously rising quickly*) May I say something, my Lord?
Judge Yes.

Casely sits

Highwood Regarding your allegation that I was "searching for a chance to expose the views of Mrs Casely". I was not. I only ——
Judge I have told you that I will deal with your contempt later.
Highwood What I have to say affects the main issue here. Now. (*He takes a moment*) As I was saying, I only exposed her views to restore the balance after she had exposed my views on what she called mercy-killing. I simply retaliated. I did not try to subvert the course ——
Judge Your views on the matter may be pertinent to the jury. Hers are not.
Highwood That's only your opinion, isn't it. She ——
Judge No, it is *not* my opinion. It is a matter of the rules of evidence ——
Highwood It seems to me a matter of fairness ——
Judge — and you were deliberately breaking them.
Highwood — and the pressure you are putting on me now is unfair and *you know it.*
Judge (*taking a breath; pausing*) I've already warned you once. Be careful how you conduct yourself. I have the power to ——
Highwood And that further threat from you merely demonstrates to the jury the unfairness of which I am complaining, so there doesn't seem to be much profit for you in waving your power at me, does there?

Silence

Judge (*quietly furious*) Your remarks have been noted. Now sit down and we will continue.

Highwood I still haven't made my point.

Judge Nevertheless, we will cont ——

Highwood (*continuing at his own expense*) And if I were an expensive QC and not just a defendant-in-person you'd let me make the point fully, without interruption.

Silence. Highwood swallows nervously

Judge I have the power to have you removed if I deem it necessary to the proper order of this hearing. And we will continue without you. Is that clear?

Highwood Yes.

Judge So. As this trial is the gravest possible matter for you I shall let you say what you will, briefly, weigh its value and bear your continued interruption in mind when I come to consider the matter of contempt. And if you disrupt matters again I will remove you. Proceed.

Highwood Now I can't even think straight after that.

Judge Do you wish to proceed or not?

Highwood Yes, yes. Give me a moment. You're very frightening, you know. You don't realize what power you wield.

Judge I think I do.

Highwood I meant over my mind not ... the other sort. (*He pulls himself together*) My point was that you misunderstood my attempt to "expose Mrs Casely's views". As for your untrue accusation that I ... (*he looks at his notes*) "staged a display of apparently sincere indignation", well, as we all know, judges allow any old hack junior counsel to do that all the time. Outbursts of synthetic, barristerial emotion are common currency in these courts. They are all part of the games you lawyers play with other people's lives. That's why Mrs Casely's private views are so relevant to the jury: she's been appointed so that when she has to wax indignant, her professional stance will have the maximum possible sincere input.

Judge Thank you, Mr Highwood. I shall record your complaint about my handling of this case, and note, on the matter of contempt, that you have again persisted in attacking Mrs Casely in spite of my earlier instruction. Now may we continue?

Ackroyd looks suicidal

Highwood As long as the jury realize that you have no views, or take no sides, on the matter of my sincerity or honesty.

Judge I don't and I am sure they do. (*He changes gear quite quickly*) Now. It is my duty to tell you that if you object to my handling of this case it could be grounds for any appeal you may wish to make should you be found guilty.

Highwood (*smiling*) You mean go and complain about one judge to another judge?

Judge It is your right.

Highwood It is also my right to slit my throat but I'm not exercising it.

Judge I have explained the procedure to you.

Highwood Thank you.

Judge (*smiling grimly*) And perhaps I should inform you, as well, that you do not have the right to slit your throat while you're in the custody of the Crown. Yes. Mrs Casely?

Casely (*standing*) Now then, Mr Highwood, regarding your sincerity, I should like to evaluate that commodity. Do you have any objection?

Highwood None. From you I expect it. It's another thing coming from the Judge, who's supposed to be neutral.

Ackroyd (*muttering*) Oh, God.

Judge (*with a glint of humour*) Are you all right, Mr Ackroyd?

Ackroyd (*standing*) Sorry, my Lord. (*He sits*)

Casely Now then, Mr Highwood, let us see where we are. You say you are opposed to mercy-killing, yet you kill your helpless, inn — your son — in precisely that way. You ask us to believe it was all on impulse and would the jury please call it manslaughter, not murder.

Highwood I have simply told you what happened and I ask the jury to define that as manslaughter.

Casely How very ingenuous of you, Mr Highwood. Now, I'm going to explain something to you then ask you a question. In law, manslaughter is the unlawful taking of another person's life, but *without intent to kill*. The additional ingredient in murder is the intent to kill or cause grievous bodily harm. That is the essential difference, even if you're sorry afterwards. If you meant it it cannot be manslaughter. Do you see? That is the law.

Highwood So you say.

Casely That is the common law of this country, upheld by Parliament.

Highwood But Parliament is not trying me. These twelve people here are. *They* will tell you what the law is, Mrs Casely, not Parliament, nor your law books, nor your legal experts. And it was Parliament who decided it would be that way.

Casely I'm afraid not, Mr Highwood. The jury decides what the facts are, but they are bound by the law like anyone else.

Highwood No. They *are* the law, just for this trial. You and I are bound by it, but they *are* it. Your wigs and gowns and paraphernalia and all the authority of that judge are powerless before their verdict and I urge them to remember that. (*He turns to the jury*) You may decide *anything*, as you wish. You have had that power for hundreds of years.

Casely I said I was going to explain something to you then ask you a question. My explanation was of the difference in law between murder and manslaughter. My question is: did you understand that difference before this trial?

Highwood I understand that lawyers make that distinction. I am also positive that they are wrong, and my distinction — that the jury will decide the difference — is right.

Casely Thank you. And there we have, you see, what I call your strategy-of-murder. You have committed this crime, you have no choice but to admit to it, it is what it is, yet you are hoping to try to get the jury to call it something else.

Highwood Wrong. Whatever the jury call it, that's what it will be.

Casely Did you intend to kill your son when you put that pillow over his head?

Silence

Highwood I can't remember.

Casely Come on, Mr Highwood. This is not an everyday occurrence, is it? Try to remember.

Highwood I can't.

Casely Well you weren't trying merely to injure him, were you?

Highwood I can't remember.

Casely So you must have been trying to kill him.

Highwood It was just black.

Casely And trying so hard, you kept that pillow down, while your baby kicked out his life, for certainly two, and possibly three, minutes.

Highwood What has time to do with it?

Casely And in your efforts to get the jury to call it manslaughter out of sympathy, you are *lying* to us about the facts.

With this the gloves are finally fully off for Casely

Highwood Am I?

Casely "In a fit of black despair I killed him." *You planned the whole thing.* From the moment — no, from soon after, very soon after, your child was born — you planned his murder, didn't you?

Highwood If I'd planned it, I wouldn't have done it like that, would I?

Casely Oh? How would you have done it, then?

Highwood I don't know, I never got that far. But something less — awful than that was.

Casely What is the name of your son?

Highwood (*surprised*) What?
Casely Your son: his name?
Highwood Tommy.
Casely No, not your oldest child, the one you killed.

Silence

Well?
Highwood We never had him christened.
Casely Christened, no. Not you. But you must have given him a name.

Highwood shakes his head numbly

Well, what did you enter on his birth certificate?
Highwood (*barely audibly*) Nothing.
Casely What did you call your brain-damaged son, Mr Highwood?

Silence

Didn't you call him anything?

Highwood shakes his head

Well, what did Tommy and his sister call him?
Highwood Baby.
Casely And he was nine months old when you killed him. How old is your newest son, Matthew?
Highwood Four months.
Casely And yet you've given him a name long since. Why didn't you name your disabled child?

Highwood just shakes his head

You never accepted him, did you? Or his right to take his place in your family? In your flawless ... faultless ... just-so family?

Silence

Have I read you correctly, Mr Highwood? The brilliant commentator on public affairs, with his beautiful wife and perfect children. Then this birth, this poor creature whom you won't acknowledge. But you can put it right, can't you? You're above the law. You can play God with your child's life then sail away scot-free where other mere mortals would be sucked down into the quagmire of crime and punishment. You'll dispense with pedestrian barristers, represent yourself and convince the jury over the Judge's head ——

Judge Mrs Casely, you know as well as I do that how Mr Highwood chooses to be represented is no part of this hearing. It's tiresome enough having the defendant trying it on every five minutes without you joining in.

Casely I'm much obliged, my Lord. Well? Haven't I got it right? He was an encumbrance, wasn't he? A nuisance. A blemish.

Highwood (*angrily*) He was a person, for God's sake. Even *he* had a character. But a person so damaged, that ... (*he shakes his head and his voice dies away*)

Casely You decided to get rid of him yourself.

Highwood (*wearily, shaking his head again*) No.

Casely All right, so you killed your son on impulse. Then you must be sorry that you did it. Are you.

Highwood shakes his head

Does that mean you're not sorry?

Highwood It means I don't know.

Casely Well, are you glad, then?

Highwood Huh.

Casely Do you wish he was back?

Highwood shakes his head again

What does that shake mean?

Highwood (*faintly*) No, no, no.

Casely So, you don't know if you're glad or sorry but you do know you don't want him back.

Highwood He's better gone, I'm afraid.

Casely Ah, the cry of the mercy-killer. So, not a lot of remorse for your action, then.

Highwood I didn't say that.

Casely You *do* feel remorse?

Highwood I feel a turmoil of emotions. Every day. All the time.

Casely In which you can carefully hide, as you are now, the true facts about your action. You're sorry, all right. Sorry you're here facing this, not sorry that you killed your son or you would want him back, wouldn't you?

Highwood shakes his head and mutters

What?

Highwood I said, it was hopeless.
Casely And your wife, does she want him back?
Highwood What?
Casely Has she forgiven you?
Highwood Forgiven ...?
Casely For killing her baby.
Highwood Oh ... yes. Yes ... I don't know.
Casely (*surprised*) You don't know.
Highwood I think so.
Casely You think so?
Highwood She says so.
Casely And does she mean it?
Highwood I think — I presume — I — that's what I don't know.
Casely You don't know?
Highwood (*losing control*) Oh, stop trying to apply normal standards. "I killed her baby", as though I were a monster who kills babies on a whim. *He* was ... we're only here because this whole thing is desperately abnormal.
Casely *He* was ... what, Mr Highwood?

There is no answer

"He was the monster", you were going to say.
Highwood No, no, no, I would die before I would say that.
Casely In this court, perhaps, but you thought it.
Highwood I — we — thought fifty different things in as many seconds, don't you see? You cannot understand what we went through. If you could you wouldn't stand there doing what you're doing now. You'd crawl away in shame.
Casely (*stung*) You took away your child's life, Mr Highwood. That's what I'm doing here: prosecuting you for that.
Highwood He — it — everything — was hopeless.
Casely *In your view.* And when he was gone, it was a load off your mind.
Highwood (*laughing disbelievingly*) A load off my — oh, God.
Casely I've got it right, haven't I? His birth was the cause of your pain; his death the relief from it.
Highwood (*fiercely*) They were both the cause. Yes, his death was a relief, too, in a way, but that redoubles the torture.
Casely Why is that? Guilt? Remorse at your crime?
Highwood I don't know. I haven't analysed it. I can't. Not yet.
Casely Another subject on which you have written at some length is: the equality of the sexes. You've actually written reams on the subject. (*She holds up two books*) You do believe all this, do you?

Highwood Of course I do.

Casely And yet you made the ultimate decision about your son's existence without a word to his mother.

Highwood How could I when ——

Casely Not a word? Not a hint?

Highwood — I didn't know I was going to.

Casely When the chips were down, your dismissal of your wife's, his mother's, rights was total, wasn't it?

Highwood What I did was on impulse.

Casely (*suddenly changing tack*) Or am I barking up the wrong tree? Are you covering up for her? Was it she who actually did it?

Silence

Yes, of course. Either you planned it or you're covering up for her. And I don't think you planned it alone, because you would never have deprived her of her rights. It is utterly out of your character. You would have had to tell her. Are you here in her place?

This scores. After a moment Highwood goes to speak but changes his mind

What? Yes?

Highwood Do I have to listen to this?

Judge Counsel is following a perfectly proper line.

Highwood But she's suggesting my wife did it.

Judge Or was at least involved. Which I am sure she's coming to next.

Casely Quite so, my Lord.

Judge Mrs Casely is treading a well-worn path.

Highwood I wouldn't expect her to be original.

Judge Mrs Casely?

Casely Yes. You wouldn't do it without her, nor she without you. Two articulate liberals who would discuss every detail of their life together and their children's lives — or death. You would have *had* to talk about this first. We share everything, even ... That is what happened, isn't it, Mr Highwood?

Silence

Judge Answer the question, Mr Highwood.

Highwood It's not worth answering.

Judge But you must.

Highwood Must? Must? I refuse.

Casely I'll assume a denial, my Lord.

Judge Inferences may be drawn by the jury, Mr Highwood.

Highwood (*blurting it out*) My wife is not involved in any way. In fact I was careful to make sure that she ——

Casely (*quietly*) You were careful to make sure that she what, Mr Highwood?

Highwood (*mind racing*) After I — did it, I was careful to make sure that ——

Casely Yes?

Highwood — she ... didn't ——

Casely Well?

Highwood — wasn't ... involved.

Casely But she wasn't, anyway.

Highwood I mean, that she wasn't thought to be involved.

Casely Why should anyone think she was involved when she wasn't?

Highwood You've just demonstrated that.

Casely Really? How?

Highwood By suggesting we were in it together.

Casely But how were you careful to make sure that nobody thought she was involved?

Highwood What?

Casely How, Mr Highwood?

Highwood How, what ... ? (*He is utterly lost and confused*)

Casely Well? What did you do? What steps did you take?

Highwood I didn't.

Casely But you just said that you did.

Highwood I mean, I couldn't. I tried but I failed.

Casely You're not making sense, Mr Highwood.

Highwood After I — had done it — I realized I must defend my wife from pain. I told her she was not involved. I told her Cabby was better off, that he'd thank us — in person, one day. It was no good. She was — she felt — well ...

Casely Mr Highwood, it's another smoke-screen, isn't it?

Highwood No.

Casely It bears no relevance to what you just said.

Highwood Yes it does.

Casely And who is Cabby, Mr Highwood?

Highwood (*shocked to the core*) What?

Casely You just mentioned Cabby.

Highwood Did I?

Casely Yes. He was better off, you said. He would thank you both one day — in person.

Highwood Cabby was — our son.

Casely So that was your name for him. Why Cabby?

Highwood Private.

Casely You won't tell us?

Highwood None of your business.

Judge Mr Highwood, it is your duty to give a full and accurate account at this stage. You won't have another opportunity.

Highwood (*further undermined*) He was called Cabby one day by accident and it stuck. There. Is that accurate enough for you?

Judge Mrs Casely?

Casely So the name Cabby meant nothing, a slip of the tongue?

Highwood Yes. Yes and no.

Casely Nothing you say means nothing.

Highwood Nothing and everything. Sometimes you just want something to mean nothing.

Casely It sounds like a diminutive to me, Mr Highwood. Don't you agree?

There is no answer

If you had to shorten something to Cabby, what would it be? Any suggestions, Mr Highwood?

Again, no answer

Can't you even hazard a guess for us?

Highwood (*bitterly*) I'm sure you've managed without me.

Casely (*discovering it*) Cabbage. That's a possibility, don't you think? Cabbage. How apt.

Highwood (*nearly out of control*) It didn't mean what you're now going to try and make it mean.

Casely I do not wish to try and make it mean anything, Mr Highwood. I am just a barrister doing my job, seeking the truth.

Highwood Oh, is that all you are?

Casely Every grain of which I have to winkle out of you. The jury will remember with great clarity your story of the moment when you realized your son was a vegetable. They will recall that you stumbled over the word, nearly broke down, then got it out and informed us that it was the first time you'd managed to say it. It was a relief. Now what do we learn? That you'd been going round gaily calling him Cabbage for months.

Highwood Gaily.

Casely And now we have the emotional cover-up again as I get to the heart of your relationship — or lack of it — with your unfortunate son.

Highwood (*pouring this out*) It was the first time I'd got the word vegetable out *in public* I said. The name Cabby was intensely private, and when Jean first said it, it was an accident, she fell over it in a way, and it became an endearment that I was glad to use, not an insult, it was a relief, a ... oh, you don't even want to understand. (*He is only just hanging on*)

Casely And out of that emotional smoke-screen I hear that Cabbage doesn't mean what it clearly does and that "it wasn't me, my Lord, it was my wife wot done it".

Highwood That was a compliment to her, not an accusation.

Casely Why would Cabby thank you *both*, in person, Mr Highwood?

Highwood What?

Casely For killing him? Your words were "he'd thank us — in person, one day." Why us? Why not you alone?

Highwood I wanted to involve her.

Casely Just now you said, "I was careful to make sure that she *wasn't* involved." Now you want to involve her. Which version would you like the jury to believe?

Highwood Both are true.

Casely Mr Highwood, your story is falling apart at the seams.

Highwood I wanted to keep the family together.

Casely Having killed one member of it.

Highwood To keep the remaining members together.

Casely You're an atheist, so your writings tell us.

Highwood A humanist: I believe in man as a responsible and progressive intellectual being.

Casely Oh, yes. I see. An optimist. (*From a press clipping*) I quote: "a person who believes there's a God will believe anything?" Still think that?

Highwood I don't bother God and he doesn't bother me.

Casely Yet you said Cabby would thank you both in person one day. What are your wife's beliefs, Mr Highwood?

Highwood You must ask her.

Casely But I can't, she's not giving evidence, is she, Mr Highwood. You haven't called her. (*She shrugs in mock helplessness*) So there you were: *in extremis* following your unpremeditated act of killing; trying to involve your wife having carefully ensured she wasn't involved; so confused that you can't remember precisely what you meant by certain very clearly expressed phrases; you picked up your dead son and, in a state of intense mental and emotional shock, you took him to hospital. Is all that right? Is it right?

Highwood You put it so —— (*He searches for something to say*)

Casely Yet you managed to remember to take some sleeping tablets with you so that you could pass a peaceful night in the cells.

Highwood stares at her

Just another little instinctive, spontaneous act, eh? Almost involuntary, really. Any of us would have done it.

Highwood Er — yes.

Casely What made you think of sleeping tablets, Mr Highwood, in the state you were in?

Highwood I ... what?

Casely The sleeping tablets: what made you think of taking them with you?

Highwood I can't — I'm not ——

Casely What were your first words to the doctor in casualty when you arrived there — in deep shock — with your dead child's body?

Highwood My first what?

Casely Let me remind you. They were, according to Doctor Bannerjee's statement — (*she holds it up*), "Am I too late? Can he be a donor?" Is that right?

Highwood just groans

(*Reading*) "I am his father. I give my consent". Another unpremeditated idea, eh? When the doctor said no, you said, "Can't you use his heart, his lungs, anything?" It was the one thing you showed any feeling about, the doctor says. "His liver? Not even his eyes for some kid who needs them?" Did you think Cabby's parts were more useful than Cabby?

Highwood They said ... they said ...

Casely Yes?

Highwood (*faintly*) No ... post-mortem, you see ...

Casely What made you think of taking the sleeping tablets with you to the hospital?

Highwood Wha ...?

Casely The sleeping tablets?

Highwood groans

What made you think of taking them to the hospital?

Another noise from Highwood

Casely Mr Highwood, are you listening to ——

Highwood (*starting to fall completely apart*) It was a Tuesday. I took him to the hospital in the car.

Casely Come, come, Mr Highwood do keep calm. Would you like a glass of water?

Highwood (*tears streaming down his face; utterly lost*) He was on the front seat beside me.

Casely Mr Highwood, taking sleeping tablets to the hospital to ensure that
  you don't have a restless night and offering your dead son's body for spare-
  part surgery were the coherent, sane acts of a man in charge of his ——
Judge Mrs Casely, I don't wish to interrupt.
Casely My Lord.
Judge Mr Highwood, are you all right? Can you continue?
Highwood Wha...?
Judge Mrs Casely, has asked you a question: how did you remember to —— ?

From the back of the auditorium, we hear Jean's voice

Jean (*off; shouting*) I gave him the bloody sleeping tablets. I saw the state
  he was in so I shoved them in his pocket.
Judge ⎱ (*together*) ⎰ Remove that person from the court, will you ?
Jean ⎰   ⎱ Can't you see he's had enough? Let the poor
                         man ——

A door slams

Judge Mr Highwood. You have not answered ——

*He is interrupted by a terrible sound. It is Highwood drawing in the first of
a series of great, audible, scraping breaths as he breaks down. He does this
several times before, eventually, to his own and everyone's relief, it develops
into sobbing of a more orthodox and bearable manner*

  Ladies and gentlemen, we will adjourn for some minutes until Mr
  Highwood recovers his composure.

Highwood continues to sob

  Mr Ackroyd, see that Mr Highwood has some medical attention. The court
  is adjourned.

*The Judge and Casely quickly leave and Ackroyd helps the shaking,
convulsed Highwood off*

Black-out

CURTAIN

ACT II

Some minutes later

Jean and Highwood are downstage in the cell. The courtroom is in darkness

Highwood So that's what a nervous breakdown is. You just stop. (*He smiles*) I didn't feel a thing, just frozen, I mean immobilized. Casely seemed to be punching holes in me. Did I say anything?

Jean You just stood and cried. That was all.

Highwood First of all I couldn't think fast enough, then, I couldn't think at all. I really didn't say anything?

Jean No, nothing.

Highwood It was all whirling round in my head.

Jean Jeremy thinks we should get a top QC.

Highwood (*in a sudden, agonized rage*) No, no, *no*. He'll fuck it up. He'll rely on the law. We'll be fighting appeals, civil servants, social workers, the House of Lords; it'll be a complete fuck-up. I've seen it all. A hundred times. No. You can't trust 'em. You can trust a jury — perhaps. Anyway, they're all we have. I'll sort out the jumble in my head. Honestly, darling. I will. Who does Jeremy suggest we get? (*His rage has drained away. He has nearly fallen apart again*)

Jean He says Piers Staunton will be a match for Casely.

Highwood A match. That's what they understand, don't they, lawyers? On my left, Margaret Casely, QC, the heavyweight champion and representative of religious reaction. On my right, Piers Staunton, civilized, quiet-spoken; loves ballet but packs a tremendous punch. Never mind that there's some defendant, whose life their exquisitely-matched battle will change forever, the law can function as it knows how.

The cell door off stage opens

Ackroyd enters

Ackroyd I've got the doctor to order you to hospital under guard. For tests. We're adjourned for a week.

Jean Thank God. Come on.

Ackroyd No. Sorry, Jean. Not you. Not in the police van.

Jean Trust there to be some regulation.

Ackroyd No, no, it's security. You go out of another exit later. They've got a different car for you. It's a shambles out front; media, demonstrators. Haven't they got anything better to do? There's even a prayer meeting. They're saying God has struck you down.

Highwood Look after yourself, darling.

Jean And you. See you soon.

Highwood starts to go

Ackroyd James. You're on a sort of parole in a way. You won't — um — well, of course, you won't try to — um ——

Highwood What?

Ackroyd Well ... escape.

Highwood (*amazed*) Where to? What for?

Ackroyd Sorry. I was instructed to say it.

Highwood exits

Jean So we're going to lose, are we?

Ackroyd Look at him. He's barely fit to walk, let alone ... of course, that might help us at the appeal.

Jean (*impatiently*) How long will I have to be without him?

Ackroyd (*shaking his head*) Life is the sentence. But — well, some years in practice. It's mandatory.

Jean They should give him a medal, not this.

Ackroyd (*annoyed; upset*) Jean, he's committed a ... and his defence is so *pointless*. Just an appeal to turn a blind eye, really.

Jean An appeal for common sense.

Ackroyd It has no basis in law or morality or ——

Jean In anything, except common sense.

Ackroyd So, parents everywhere have the right to —— ?

Jean Oh, why drag in a rash of hypothetical — parents aren't going to start killing their children because of — this is purely our business.

Ackroyd No, Jean, it's not and you know it. The law is not just some abstract idea. It's there to protect us all. Anyway, this case is such a high-profile affair now. The whole country is divided over it.

Jean With most on our side, according to the polls.

Ackroyd That won't help him in this courtroom.

Jean Oh, Jeremy. I know. Of course I do.

Ackroyd He should have pleaded guilty, kept his head down, got Piers Staunton to beg for mercy, and later on, got the maximum remission.

Jean The rich man's way.

Ackroyd Yes, yes, well, he is rich. Piers Staunton would *use* all this medical stuff. He'd find a way through the law to *help* James instead of ——

Jean We'll call a QC in for any appeal that is necessary — *if* one is ——

Ackroyd It will be, Jean. Make no mistake.

Jean Oh, stop assuming he's lost before it's ——

Ackroyd Jean, he *doesn't stand* a chance against Casely.

Jean (*suddenly*) Oh, to hell with Casely. Don't you realize it was me who did it?

Ackroyd What?

Jean It was me. I did it. Not James.

Ackroyd What?

Jean Thank God I've said it to someone at last.

Ackroyd You ——?

Jean *Yes*. Wake *up*, Jeremy.

Ackroyd You mustn't tell me things that I'm not supposed to ——

Jean Oh, Jeremy. Let all that go. It was me. And it was on impulse.

Ackroyd I wondered, you know, I often wondered. Then I decided it couldn't have been you.

Jean Why not?

Ackroyd You could have got away with it. Infanticide, not murder. A mother can commit infanticide with no mandatory sentence but not a father.

Jean He had taken my place before we knew all that. I was seven months' pregnant. He wouldn't hear of me giving myself up. He'd confessed before I even ... it was done; the thing was set in cement. He said he'd be charged with manslaughter not murder and he'd get himself off somehow. He's been wrong about everything.

Ackroyd Oh, what a dreadful mess.

Jean That's why he won't even call me to give evidence. He knows I'll blow it all.

Ackroyd Perhaps, if you confessed now.

Jean I was going to. Months ago. Jimmy stopped me. He nearly went mad. He'd already confessed, he said. If I did, too, it would look like collusion. Partners in crime. The children could lose us both — possibly be taken away from us for good. Someone might argue — some child welfare official — that they were in danger from us. That frightened me. Jimmy said the children, especially Matthew, needed me for the next few years, more than him, so I — I went along with — God, I wish I hadn't.

Ackroyd Well, then, I don't know, perhaps you should conf — no, no, you must keep quiet — no, I didn't say that. I mean, I — um — oh dear. I'm in an impossible position.

Jean If we had suspected when I was pregnant, Cabby would have been aborted and no law would have been broken. Cabby, that poor little thing ...

Ackroyd This trial, this whole — it's all a sham — an irrelevance.

Jean I held him and fed him.

Ackroyd What?

Jean My son.

Ackroyd What happened?

Jean All that Jimmy said in there was true about doing it on impulse. It was just that it was my impulse, not his. He came into the room, you know, just as I was — he didn't realize for a while. He thought Cabby was having a fit or something and I was holding him down. He had these violent, threshing ... By the time he realized, it was done. He stood shaking like a leaf, teeth chattering, sobbing, shocked to pieces. I had to hold him tight. Oh, he can take the blame, he's got that sort of courage, but ... when Casely said to him "Has your wife forgiven you?", I nearly screamed. The point is: has he forgiven me? He's gone to gaol for me but does he think it's worth it? That eats me. Oh, he thought of doing it hims — but Jimmy's the great arguer, the man of ideas, he could never push the button. And none of what I have just told you is the difficult bit, the really difficult bit. Now, I'm at home, by myself, with guilt, alone. I can't talk to anyone. I killed my baby and I must keep it to myself. I didn't know the world could be so lonely. Jimmy's the public figure, with something to do, in court, arguing to the whole country, hated and loved. I sit in the public gallery nursing my — crime? Is it the word?

Jeremy No, no.

Jean Six months. I've talked to no-one. I sometimes feel that I'll fall apart, into shreds, be blown away, de-materialize completely. All anyone can talk about is how to fight this case. I'm not allowed to even ... pressure? Huh. He falls apart in public and the nation says "poor man". I am granted no such luxury. Do you know how inadequate you feel bringing Cabby into the world? And then how guilty you feel when you remove him from it?

Highwood enters

Highwood I worked on the doctor who worked on security. They think you'll be safer in a police van. Fancy a ride with me?

Jean I've told him.

Highwood What?

Jean Everything.

Highwood (*to Ackroyd*) It's not true.

Jean What's not true?

Highwood What?

Jean How do you know something's not true when you don't even know what it is?

Highwood I don't understand.
Jean Oh, Jimmy. He knows. Everything. Drop it.

Highwood stands, swaying

Ackroyd It's all right, James. I — um — she was overwrought, I didn't hear what — I didn't *believe* what she said.
Highwood How could you? You promised.
Jean It's another mind. On our side.
Highwood It's another mouth.

Black-out; immediately, there is the clang of a cell door closing

In the darkness, Highwood and Jean exit

The Lights come up on a downstage area as:

Casely enters, expansive and sure

Casely Ah, Ackroyd. Here we are again, ready for the fray. Your client is fully recovered, I trust, after his week's rest?
Ackroyd As well as can be expected.
Casely Yes. Quite, quite. Let us hope there are no sudden relapses should I approach the truth too closely again.
Ackroyd Unlikely.
Casely (*smiling*) I won't ask which of those two eventualities you think is unlikely.
Ackroyd Quite. Good-morning, Mrs ... (*He starts to go*)
Casely No, no, no, no, no. Just a moment. Let's have a sensible word. Without prejudice, of course.
Ackroyd Well?
Casely I want you — and your clients — to know — that I think this whole thing is most regrettable.
Ackroyd I'm sure they'll be choked with gratitude to hear that.
Casely But we can't have people going round committing murder and getting away with it, can we? Not even doting dads ... or mums.

Silence

I mean, we none of us know the full facts, do we?
Ackroyd The facts are as my client has stated them.

Casely Oh, yes, yes, of course. But I mean *the full, true facts*.

Ackroyd What do you want, Mrs Casely?

Casely Ah. Yes. Highwood has made this trial most high-profile. You can read, hear or watch nothing else. People can't manœuvre quietly in private. We're all pushed into fixed positions.

Ackroyd Are we?

Casely So silly. Futile. First of all he's asserting a man's right to take life. What a crusade. Hopeless.

Ackroyd I don't think he's asserting a person's right to take life or any other crusade.

Casely I didn't say a person's, I said a man's ... rather different.

Pause

Ackroyd Well?

Casely The law, as we know, is absolutely adamant. A person's right to life is sacrosanct, inalienable. *You may not take another person's life ... (She pauses, then continues quite quickly)* Except in war, accidents, self-defence, if your husband or wife provokes you enough, if you're the public executioner and several other sets of mitigating circumstances. The law is very wise ... wiser than some think.

Ackroyd Highwood thinks it's an ass.

Casely Yes, I'd detected a certain lack of faith.

Ackroyd Well?

Casely And besides challenging the right to life to all Her Majesty's subjects ...

Ackroyd Bar the exceptions you mentioned ——

Casely Quite — he has mounted a challenge to test who runs Her Majesty's legal system. He's not doing too badly for one little, domestic murderer, is he?

Ackroyd Highwood has always been an achiever.

Casely I suppose it's too late to persuade your man to get properly represented, is it? I'm sure — um — Piers Staunton, for instance, would drop everything if you asked him.

Ackroyd Piers Staunton? I don't know.

Casely Piers and I get on, you know. I'm sure we could've managed something.

Ackroyd However, it's me you have to deal with.

Casely So be it. I'm very reasonable, you know.

Ackroyd This is a criminal case, not a civil one, there's nothing we can settle at the courtroom door.

Casely Absolutely. My word. Yes. Quite, Quite. Hm. Let us suppose that *she* did it.

Silence

No comment to make? She's the mother, the child was under a year old. It's infanticide.

Ackroyd But it's not her, is it?

Casely But if it were, and she confessed, and he owned up that he'd only said he did it to protect her, then we'd have a very different trial, wouldn't we? And she'd get off. Then everyone'd be happy. Especially your clients.

Ackroyd You obviously don't like the way things are going.

Casely I detest the way things are going. Going? They've gone. They're already a bloody disaster.

Ackroyd I'm talking about the result.

Casely Oh, that. That'll be a disaster, all right — for your client. And *I* don't necessarily want a conviction either. We don't want a martyr over such a self-evidently unsuitable precedent. But I'm not going to let him get away with it. Why does he have to take on the entire religious and legal establishment at once? Wouldn't one at a time do?

Ackroyd (*carefully*) Sometimes people see themselves trapped, with no choices.

Casely Ah. Feels trapped, does he? Let's spring it for him.

Ackroyd How?

Casely By getting his wife to own up.

Ackroyd I beg your pardon.

Casely I mean confess.

Ackroyd Even though she's innocent.

Casely She could save her husband.

Ackroyd You're suggesting that I should ——

Casely Oh, yes, yes, yes, never mind that. Can't we do *something*?

Pause

Ackroyd I'll see.

Casely Well, do your best. You sounded just then like a man with something on your mind. Bring it out. Come on, what is it? It may help. She is involved in some way, isn't she?

Ackroyd (*offended*) Your cheap cross-examination tricks do not take me in, I assure you.

Casely Of course they don't, old chap. Like to see a man's calibre though.

Ackroyd And don't patronize me either, I might want to instruct you one day.

Casely Let's never forget *that*. Clients come and go but we're in this game together, aren't we? Now, will you come with me to the Judge?

Ackroyd Whatever for?

Casely Don't worry, I'll do all the talking, it's my neck on the block, but it would be improper for me to see him without you there. We don't want a mis-trial, do we? And I need his OK to drop in on your client. If he'll see me.

Ackroyd We'd better tell the Judge's clerk to hold things up for a while.

Casely Absolutely. Oh, by the way, should you want to instruct me one day, I'd just like to say — in all diffidence — my cross-examination tricks are not cheap. Come on.

Black-out

Casely exits; Jean and Highwood enter

The Lights come up on Jean, Highwood and Ackroyd in the downstage area representing the cell

Ackroyd (*apologetically, but sticking to his guns*) James, listen to me: Casely was sure that it was Jean before we spoke. Oh, it was never said in so many words but that's why she made the offer. She's trying to help. She may detest your views but she's entirely honourable.

Highwood reacts

Yes, she is. And she's taking quite a risk on your behalf. She wants the truth to out but until you and Jean co-operate no-one can move. There's no evidence anywhere except your words. You should have heard the conversation in there: the Judge and Casely skating round the subject for all their worth, neither saying what they thought. Oh, the Judge is totally pissed off with you, ostensibly for your behaviour in court but I think it's because he's guessed the truth too and he's sure you've set yourself up against the law. And that would be a real contempt. But he's still willing to help. So is Casely. At least hear her offer.

Highwood OK, find Casely, would you? Only one thing: you mustn't speak while we're together. Sorry, Jeremy, but that's an instruction.

Ackroyd All right.

Ackroyd goes

Jean Am I allowed to open *my* mouth, then?

Highwood We mustn't contradict one another.

Jean But I want to own up and you don't want me to. How do we reconcile that?

Silence

(*Crying out*) How do you think I feel?
Highwood If you hadn't done it when you did, I would have.
Jean No, no, no.
Highwood I'd thought about it for ages.
Jean Oh, yes. I believe that.

Ackroyd enters

Ackroyd Right. Casely's outside now. The Judge knows we're talking and
will wait.
Highwood Sorry, you're too soon. We still haven't sorted ourselves out.
Ackroyd Oh, well, I think you must ——
Highwood Please, Jeremy, just wait outside and make sure that door is
closed and Casely can hear nothing. We'll call you.
Ackroyd Yes, all right, but you ——
Highwood And, Jeremy, please don't even chat to her.
Ackroyd (*offended, but ploughing on*) You can't start having a heart-to-
heart now.
Jean (*impatiently*) Oh, Jeremy, just tell her to wait.
Ackroyd I'll do my best.

He exits

Highwood Listen, darling, listen. You must understand ... what you did was —
not wrong.
Jean Why don't you say it was right?
Highwood I can't. But it's still not wrong.
Jean (*emotionally*) Just tell me that you hate me and I can deal with it. I can't
cope with "not wrong".

Highwood is stunned

Highwood Of course I don't hate ——
Jean I saw *you* draw back from doing it; twice actually.
Highwood It seemed like a rebuke, a rejection of you and what you had
produced.
Jean *We* produced, surely.
Highwood In the end Cabby came out of *you* and I couldn't do it — against
you.
Jean Oh, no, Jimmy, no. That's not true. You could never have done it
anyway. But I did ... And now we're strangers.

There is a knock off stage and the sound of the cell window sliding open

Ackroyd (*off*) James. Jean. Are you ready yet?
Highwood (*calling*) No.
Ackroyd (*off*) The whole court's waiting you know.
Highwood (*calling*) Two more minutes. We've got to get the tactics right.
Jean (*starting to crack*) Let me confess. Please. We didn't foresee this offer.
   It might get us both off.
Highwood (*distraught*) What offer? What are the details, the small print?
Jean (*giving way*) All right. Relax. You're right. We'll do as you say.
Highwood (*placating her*) No. no. Listen, listen, listen. Let's look at all
   possible outcomes. If you confess, we could both go free ... Or both get
   entangled in some sort of collusion or conspiracy or accessory accusation
   and lose the children, our liberty, everything. If we stay with this trial, we
   could still both go free ...
Jean (*shaking her head*) Oh, Jimmy.
Highwood BUT if things go wrong ... no matter how badly ... only *one* of
   us is trapped.
Jean You.
Highwood Not relevant.
Jean For my unilateral action.
Highwood We must keep *one* of us out of gaol. For the children.
Jean (*cracking*) Jimmy. Take her offer — any offer.
Highwood I won't let a decent chance go.
Jean (*grabbing him*) Jimmy, please, for me, take ——
Highwood Darling, please don't. If you plead with me like that I'll go to
   pieces. The children need you. (*He breaks away*)
Jean (*lost*) But I need *you*.
Highwood I can't keep this up if you — that's partly why I didn't appeal after
   that bail screw-up. I knew that months with you — I'd've caved in.

Pause

Jean Oh ... I thought you couldn't face me after what I'd ——
Highwood Oh, darling, *no*. Of course not.

*They stare at each other for a moment, then fall into each other's arms. This
is their first real relief since Cabby's death. There is a knock*

   Ready?

Jean nods

Come in.

Ackroyd and Casely enter

There is a mood of false bonhomie although Highwood is very hyped up

Ackroyd Sorry to hassle, both of you, but ...

Highwood and Jean hold each other for a while

Highwood That's all right, Jeremy, we understand. But we'd only just discovered how little time we've had together since ... um, things. Hallo. (*He nods at Casely*)

Casely How do you do, if I may say that, meeting you properly, as it were.

Highwood Yes, yes. This is my wife, Jean, who you must have ——

Casely Yes, indeed, I've seen you on the telly. And I enjoyed your timely interjection into the proceedings when your husband — um ...

Jean Blew his fuses.

Casely (*laughing*) Quite.

Highwood Yes, that's a point. Will there be any problem about Jean being re-admitted to the trial?

Casely Of course, she's been thrown out, hasn't she. Well, it's up to the Judge, but I'll try.

Jean Utter silence. I promise.

Highwood If he won't allow it, I'll demand her as my McKenzie Friend.

Casely You have your solicitor there; I'm not sure what the regulations are about further assistance from a lay person.

Highwood You have teams of them. I think I should be allowed a mere two. If the Judge refuses I shall enjoy making an issue of it.

Ackroyd Why don't you leave it to me, Casely's junior and the Judge's clerk. I am sure we can do things better between ——

Highwood I thought you weren't going to speak, Jeremy.

Ackroyd contains himself

Right. What can we do for you, Mrs Casely?

Casely (*smiling*) You do for —— ? I thought you wanted this meeting.

Highwood No.

Casely (*smoothly*) No, that's right. It was Ackroyd and I who ... well, basically, I don't want to see you go to prison for years, Mr Highwood. I don't think anyone does.

Highwood Including me.

Casely You make me wonder, the way you're handling things.

Highwood Thank you. Well, if you don't want to see me go to prison, just drop the charge. It's quite simple.

Casely A criminal law has been broken; a life has been taken; society must have its culprit. You've volunteered for that unenviable position. Most commendable, jolly brave. But if we had a different volunteer the law broken could be a different law and the volunteer's position would be far less uncomfortable, indeed, relatively tolerable.

Highwood So: my wife says she did it, I say I was covering up for her, she's only guilty of infanticide, not murder, I'm let off, she's put on probation or something, the law is satisfied and we all go home and live happily ever after.

Casely That's about it. Yes.

Highwood Even though it bears no relation to the facts.

Casely As far as we know, the facts are as you have stated them. If you and your wife say they're different, then in law they become different in the absence of any conflicting evidence. You were the only ones there.

Highwood All right. If you will just give me all that in writing — you know, in full legalese — and signed by the proper authority, it's a deal.

Casely (*laughing quietly*) You know I can't do that, don't you?

Highwood So you're not offering us that deal at all. You're offering us something rather less.

Casely I'm offering you that deal in a verbal contract.

Highwood Which, as you-know-who said, "isn't worth the paper it's written on".

Casely I have spoken to those instructing me in this matter and I feel confident of the outcome.

Highwood Well, bully for you. That's lovely, isn't it. You feel confident; we take the risk. Lovely. What guarantees have you? Cast-iron, copper-bottomed guarantees.

Casely By its very nature this must be a discreet operation but I think you may be sure that when I say that the people to whom I have spoken have assured me that they wouldn't want this matter prosecuted further ——

Highwood Suppose this deal went wrong and I was trying to sue you for breach of contract. And I stood up in court and said, "My Lord, she said that she *thinks* I *may* be sure that certain *unspecified* people have assured her that they *wouldn't want* ...". The Judge would tell me to sue myself for negligence in drawing up the contract, wouldn't he?

Casely I am obliged to phrase things like that.

Highwood Because that's all you can offer. BUT ... minds change, men in suits move on, political pressure is brought, some fool tries to bar Jean from our children for some sociological reason; or we're accused of complicity

and both end up in prison or childless. Then ... you ... none of you ... will
know anything about this deal or, if you admit you do, you'll say "It was
just a suggestion, I never had that sort of authority". It stinks.
Ackroyd (*unable to keep quiet any longer*) Nothing *can* be written or
guaranteed, James. But we all do deals like this all the time.
Highwood And when things go wrong who pays, you or your clients?

Ackroyd gestures impatiently

That question wasn't rhetorical. Who pays, you or them?
Ackroyd Nothing has ever gone wrong with any deal I've done.
Highwood My God, aren't you lucky? Or aren't your clients? In my column
and on TV I take up the cudgels for bus-loads of people for whom it went
wrong. The propensity of the legal profession to screw up is infinite. Never
gone wrong for you, Mrs Casely?
Casely It's an excellent offer. It is all I can make.
Highwood Precisely.

Silence. An impasse

Jean (*touching him*) Jimmy.

They look at each other

Highwood (*changing tack*) All right, let me put everything another way —
a more helpful way. Suppose we are both longing to accept your offer but
one of us feels insecure. Help us. Give us something to rely on.
Casely You have my word.
Highwood Thank you but something concrete to ensure that nothing will go
wrong ... further down the road.
Casely I won't necessarily be involved all the way down the road.
Highwood Precisely. So. Something in writing for when you're not there.
Casely Impossible.

Highwood shakes his head

Mrs Highwood — forgive me, this is pure hypothesis — but, if you had
done it, it would now be your duty to confess and save your husband. Your
duty.

Pause

Jean Yes. Thank you.

Casely I must warn you that the pressure you have so far experienced in that court — and under which you have already ignominiously cracked — is as nothing compared to what you have to face if you go on and are found guilty. Excuse me, that was not a threat but a friendly action to preserve you and your wife — from further unnecessary suffering.

This chills Highwood. He glances at Jean

Highwood (*quietly*) We'll take our chance with the jury.
Casely And *that* has led to many a disaster.

She exits

Highwood So now we've dealt with the truth we carry on with British justice.
Ackroyd You've left her no option. She'll only be doing her duty.
Highwood Oh, yes, where have I heard that one before.
Ackroyd I'll tell them you're coming. (*He starts to leave*)
Highwood Jeremy.

Ackroyd stops

Thank you for containing yourself.

Ackroyd nods in understanding and exits

I've done the wrong thing, haven't I?
Jean Their way sounded so safe.
Highwood I know. That's the trouble.
Jean Are you all right, darling?
Highwood No, I'm frightened. Terrified. (*He clings to her*) Come on. We've got to go.
Jean At least the jury will be able to see we're together.

The Lights change so that the whole courtroom is visible. Highwood goes to the witness-box

Casely, the Judge and Ackroyd enter and take their positions

Jean sits with Ackroyd

Judge Mr Highwood, I trust you are fully recovered.

Highwood Thank you, my Lord. I hope so.

Judge I have commented on your conduct in this court which will be dealt with in due course. I have had your wife ejected for interrupting proceedings and now I have allowed her back to be your McKenzie Friend although you have a solicitor present to guide and assist you. Mrs Casely, who has the right to object, has, generously but correctly in my view, decided not to. I have, in short, bent over backwards to accommodate you. I have done this because of the seriousness of the charge you face. I think, however, Mr and Mrs Highwood, that you should be aware that my patience is not inexhaustible. Mrs Casely.

Casely (*standing*) I, too, trust you are fully recovered, Mr Highwood.

Highwood Thank you.

Casely How exactly did you make your wife pregnant with your latest child, Matthew, Mr Highwood?

Highwood I beg your pardon?

Casely I thought I was quite clear.

Highwood Well.

Judge Are you expecting Mr Highwood to give us a lesson in elementary biology?

Casely My Lord. Mr Highwood has said her pregnancy was an accident. I mean, neither Mr nor Mrs Highwood are adolescents or virgins. They must both have extensive knowledge of birth control, yet he got her accidentally — and very conveniently — pregnant, to replace, I allege, the damaged Cabby whom he was planning to murder.

Judge Yes, yes. I see. Answer the question, Mr Highwood.

Highwood The answer is: I don't know.

Casely Oh, come now: you must have some idea.

Highwood When we realized that there was no hope for Cabby something like despair gripped us. We clung closer and closer together, both figuratively and literally. As we held each other I knew that, although fear of pregnancy was in her mind as well as mine, to mention contraception was to say the unsayable. "Shouldn't we take some precautions, darling?" Precautions against what? Another Cabby? But I knew I wanted her to be pregnant again.

Casely To replace Cabby?

Highwood No, no, no. To make us both feel ... whole again. I am sure Jean wanted it, too — needed it. But she couldn't speak either.

Casely Then how do you know she wanted it?

Highwood What?

Casely How — if she was so innocently free of any association with your crime — did you know she shared this mutual, unacknowledged wish to procreate?

Highwood Well, I guessed.

Casely Nothing adds up, does it Mr Highwood? Except that either you on your own, or you and your wife together, planned the whole thing.

Highwood (*a bit too cocky*) Or my wife on her own, don't forget that.

Pause

Casely No, that is clearly not possible, is it? Because she could have pleaded infanticide and not been on a murder charge as you now are.

Pause

Highwood Ah, no, of course. I had forgotten that, for the moment.

Casely Don't you mean again?

Judge Mrs Casely, just where is this getting us?

Casely I was exploring conspiracy, my Lord, but I now reject that because of his unguarded remark to the effect that he was careful to make sure that his wife wasn't involved. Scarcely the remark of a man who had no idea he was shortly going to kill his baby son, is it, Mr Highwood?

Highwood I'd like to explain to the jury exactly how I felt before — before it was done.

Casely At long last, Mr Highwood. An honest revelation. We are all agog.

Highwood (*to the jury*) When Cabby was — here, I used sometimes to be enraged with him. In a fury beyond reason. With this poor little thing. It was so unfair — on him I mean. I had transferred my rage at life, at nature, on to him, so ... then when I came to ... when I entered the room to ... then he was, dead. He didn't seem like a monster any more. He looked like a — baby. You see, he *looked* all right. Till he — moved ...

Casely In the middle of your account you said, "when I came to ... when I actually entered the room to ..." Not the description of an impulsive action.

Highwood Perhaps I was going in to plump up his pillow, or ... What's it matter? I was trying to tell them something important.

Casely But your sentence revealed to the jury that you had an important intention in your mind, did it not? You didn't just go into that room on impulse.

Highwood (*wearied; with contemptuous rage*) Did I do it on impulse or did I plan it? Have I got a mind or just instincts? Was I a wounded animal or a compassionate parent? What an idiotic distinction. I don't think I — or any other person on this earth — not even you — is that simple, Mrs Casely.

Casely And in the middle of all your alleged turmoil you accidentally made your wife pregnant with your shiny, new replacement for the doomed Cabby.

Highwood (*yelling; at the end of his tether*) He was still a baby, for Christ's sake, still your baby lying there. And every bit of love and protective instinct that is in you is shrieking at you to care for him. Have you thought about the frightening conflict *that* creates in you, both of you — not in me alone. What about his mother, who actually di —— (*He stops himself, just*)

Silence

Casely (*quietly*) Who actually what, Mr Highwood?

Silence

Mr Highwood, you said, "his mother, who actually di —" "Who actually did it"?

Silence

Highwood Who actually gave birth to him.
Casely But you started to say a word that began with the sound "di".
Highwood Who actually delivered him, I was going to say. Delivered him to me.

A moment's silence

Casely What extraordinary phraseology. Thank you, my Lord. That is all.
Judge Mr Highwood, you may now leave the witness-box.

Highwood leaves the witness-box

Judge We will now adjourn for a short while so the defendant may consider whether he has anything further to add to his evidence. Twenty minutes, Mr Ackroyd?
Highwood No. Nothing to add. Let's get on with it.

Black-out

Pause

In the darkness we hear Casely summing up. During her speech, the Lights come up again

Casely There is no dispute over the fact that this man killed his tiny, baby

son, and how. It was I who introduced the question of whether his wife did
it or was involved with him. But I was wrong. No evidence emerged or is
before this court of anyone other than the defendant being involved. The
defendant agrees, so that is that. The only dispute of fact is of his state of
mind. Was it a sudden act of impulse or a cold-blooded, planned affair? I
have just reviewed the evidence of the defendant and shown the gaping
holes in his story that it all happened out of the blue. You saw him, standing
there, struck dumb again and again when challenged on much vital detail
of the heart of the matter. We all sympathize with the heart-rending
circumstances of this case but a person was deprived of his life, so do not
shrink from your duty. You need not fear for the consequences to the
defendant if you find him guilty. The law is not oppressive and the learned
Judge will not, I feel sure, be without mercy in his recommendation. But
murderer he is. Even brain-damaged babies — no, I say especially brain-
damaged babies and all other defenceless members of our community —
have the right to our protection. You must not attempt to take it from them.
I do not say this man is a wicked man but he has done a wicked act; he has
wilfully taken a life and he has patently tried to cover up the truth of the
matter. That must not go unpunished. You have heard the defendant say in
this court, "I don't bother God and he doesn't bother me". Perhaps that is
at the root of this matter: faith: respect for human life; humility before God,
not the arrogance to take His decisions for Him. He also called his baby
hopelessly damaged, yet research, medicine, might suddenly come up with
anything, as it has before. Just look at the miracles of biological research.
They seem to be daily events: gene therapy, regeneration of tissue. Thus
the atheist: no faith, no hope, no charity. I remind you of those selfless,
spiritual, dedicated people who devote their lives to the disabled and find
new dimensions, joy in themselves and in their lives. But to this so-called
humanist, who claims to be a responsible and progressive being, Cabby
was not one of God's creations to cherish with love but to extinguish with
violence. Suppose his wife had another ... less-than-perfect child? No.
There is clearly no other course for you than to bring in a verdict of guilty.
One last word on his — what shall I call it? — sympathy-plea of doing it
all on impulse; a final look at his jerry-built assertion. (*She takes off her
watch*) You heard Dr Kerr, the pathologist, tell us how long it would take
for even a brain-damaged, tiny baby to die from smothering. Nearly three
minutes. I pick up the pillow — on impulse, remember, and place it over
my child's head. Go. (*She acts it out with the pillow on the exhibits table,
looking at her watch*) For a moment, say, stillness. Then the baby starts to
struggle ... possibly a cry escapes ... so harder ... the child's limbs start to
thresh ... the loving, impulsive father goes on holding down the pillow ...
the death throes of his baby reach a frenzy ... the father, still on an impulse,

still lovingly, hangs grimly on, pressing down the pillow ... The baby's movements slow down, they stop ... a few more moments for this anguished, loving father to keep his weight on the pillow to make sure — then all is still. He can relax. There. Could any one of you hold a pillow down, as I just did, for all that time, on impulse? Of course not. It was planned and executed in cold blood. (*She picks up her watch and looks at it*) And do you know how long that demonstration just took me? One minute: one third of the three minutes actually necessary.

Casely sits down. The Highwoods are both deeply shocked by this demonstration

Judge Mr Highwood?

Highwood (*standing; in shreds, barely able to speak*) It was far worse than that. My wife tells me my body ... every limb was shaking ... she's better, stronger than me. She actually changed Cabby's nappy so that he ——

Casely (*standing quickly*) My Lord, this is new evidence. I have a right ——

Judge Yes, yes, I know, I know. Mr Highwood, you cannot at this stage introduce new evid ——

Highwood My Lord, I'm sorry. I didn't mean ——

Judge I will give you the benefit. This is your last opportunity to present your case. Make proper use of it.

Highwood (*trying to pull himself together*) Yes ... right ... I ... (*He gathers himself*) Remember, a life sentence is mandatory if you find me guilty of murder. History is full of stories of juries who simply said, "What is happening here is an offence to our full, rounded head and heart; our good sense. This person, or persons, must go free." In this building is a plaque to the jury who defied a judge in sixteen seventy and found William Penn not guilty of preaching to an unlawful assembly. The judge kept them without food for two days and nights and fined them when they persisted with "not guilty". But they stood their ground and as a result William Penn went free to help build the United States of America and *you* are now the masters in this court of British justice. So, you have the power and you have the precedents. Whatever the Judge says to you, you can ignore. I urge you to do so before I even hear what it is. Mrs Casely talked of the moral dimension of the law: I agree with her. The enactment of this court should have a moral dimension; I should pay what society demands. The point is ... you are the representatives of society — not her, nor the Judge. What about the wisdom of a not guilty verdict? Will it change the law? No. I am not asking that it should be amended so that children like Cabby would lose protection. Of course we must keep that power, that sanction. My plea is simpler yet more subtle: all I am asking is that you think only of this case, no others, and ask yourselves if I have done something wrong enough for me to be gaoled for life. If you say I didn't commit a murder, then in law I didn't, no matter what the evidence is. I am not asking you to let me off. Remember, I still face — have pleaded guilty to — manslaughter. The Judge can then come into his own. He can still give me life if he thinks it right. But by using *your* discretion — by leaving me to face only the manslaughter charge — you give *him*, your servant, the chance to use *his* discretion. Good sense can then prevail. Just say "enough is enough for this man, his wife and their children". And, whatever you decide, we still have to live with these events — our own life sentence.

He sits down

Judge Ladies and gentlemen of the jury, you are here to decide the facts and only the facts, on the evidence you have heard; that is your function. Did he intend to ——
Highwood (*rising*) No, the law. You decide the *law*.

Judge } (*together*) { Highwood, you have had warnings enough.
                              Go down to the cells.
Highwood   You are the law: was it murder or manslaughter? You decide.

Judge Go down to the cells at once or I'll have you taken down.

Highwood exits

As I was saying: the facts are for the jury; the law is for the Judge. The only fact that is in dispute is intent. Did he intend to kill or not. If you are sure that he intended to kill, it is your duty to find him guilty. If you are less sure that he intended to kill his son while holding a pillow over his face for ... sufficient time, then he is guilty of the lesser charge of manslaughter. The issue is simple. Mitigating circumstances are for the Judge to determine, not you. As for his moving plea that he is somehow the exception, or above the law, that is something we hear often in these courts. It has no force. Everyone thinks they are the exception. They are not. You may now consider your verdict which at this stage of the proceedings must be unanimous.

Black-out

Highwood enters

Ackroyd and Jean move downstage

The Lights come up on the area representing the downstage cell

Highwood I've lost it, haven't I?
Ackroyd You mustn't hope for miracles.
Highwood I gave up on them after Cabby.
Ackroyd I still think Piers Staunton is the man. I mean, to lead the appeal, to work on the sentence — um — I'll just — er— you don't need ...

He exits

Highwood Well, I seem to have screwed that.
Jean I thought the Judge's summing up was quietly filthy.
Highwood He's a pro.
Jean Our lives were so beautiful.
Highwood I took it for granted. Was Casely right? Did I kill Cabby just because he didn't fit our ... image?
Jean Jimmy.
Highwood Hm?
Jean You didn't kill Cabby. I did.
Highwood Oh, God. Yes.
Jean I'm not going to be able to stand it, you know. If they send you back to prison I'm going to confess.
Highwood You mustn't. You just can't.

Ackroyd enters

Ackroyd The jury are back. Come on.

Jean and Highwood are shaken

Jean My God, that was quick. Couldn't they even pretend to ——?
Highwood Quick means bad, doesn't it? If they were going to ignore the Judge's summing up there would have bound to have been a long argument.
Ackroyd I would have thought so. Come on.

The Lights change and they take their places in the courtroom

Judge The jury have reached their verdict. I will give my judgement. James Highwood, stand up.

Highwood does so

James Highwood, the jury have found you not guilty of murder. (*He pauses for a moment*) They have, however, found you guilty of manslaughter, which I recognize you have always admitted. I am going to sentence you to two years' imprisonment. In my judgement that is the proper sentence to reflect the seriousness of the crime you have admitted. However, in view of all the exceptional circumstances, I suspend your sentence. I am taking this course because to lock you away would not be appropriate in this case, I am sure you — and, indeed, Mrs Highwood — have your own particular hells to live through. That brings me to the matter of your contempt in the face of the court. There is no doubt in my mind that you attempted, while representing yourself, to bring the due processes of law into disrepute and to subvert the course of justice. You tried more than once. Your conduct was so serious that in my view only an immediate custodial sentence is justified. You have spent six months in custody on remand. I take that into account in passing sentence on you. The sentence of the court is that you will remain in prison for a further six months to reflect on your disregard for the proper legal processes. Take him down.

The Judge, Casely and Ackroyd bow and exit

Only the Highwoods are left as the Lights fade

CURTAIN

FURNITURE AND PROPERTY LIST

Only essential items are listed here, as mentioned in the text. Further dressing may be added at the director's discretion

ACT I

On stage: Courtroom
               Bench. *On it:* judge's papers, pens, gavel, etc.
               Dock
               Lawyers' places (seats with working surfaces in front). *On them:* Casely's portable lectern, papers, press cuttings, files, brief cases, pens, etc. (**Casely, Ackroyd, Highwood**)
               Witness-box. *In it:* bible, etc.
               Exhibits table. *On it:* exhibits, including pillow, etc.

Off stage: Tray of food (**Ackroyd**)

Personal: **Ramsden**: notes
               Dr Radzinski: file
               Jean: handbag. *In it:* children's paintings
               Casely: watch

ACT II

No props required

LIGHTING PLOT

Practical fittings required: nil
Interior

ACT I

To open: Full stage lighting

Cue 1 **Judge, Casely** and **Dr Radzinski** exit (Page 10)
Crossfade to downstage area representing cell

Cue 2 **Highwood**: "The lads told me it would be." (Page 13)
Dim lights

Cue 3 **Judge** and **Casely** enter (Page 13)
Bring up full courtroom lighting

Cue 4 **Highwood** and **Ackroyd** move downstage (Page 22)
Crossfade to downstage cell area

Cue 5 **Highwood**: "He's left-handed." (Page 25)
Bring up full courtroom lighting

Cue 6 **Ackroyd** helps **Highwood** off (Page 38)
Black-out

ACT II

To open: Downstage cell area lit

Cue 7 **Highwood**: "It's another mouth." (Page 43)
Black-out

Cue 8 When ready; after the sound of the cell door closing (Page 43)
Bring lights up on a downstage area

EFFECTS PLOT

ACT I

Cue 1	As the lights crossfade to the downstage cell *Heavy metal door slam and bolt shot, off*	(Page 10)
Cue 2	**Highwood**: "I don't — think so." *Knock on cell door, off*	(Page 11)
Cue 3	**Jean**: "Oh, Jeremy, Jeremy." *Knock on cell door, off*	(Page 12)
Cue 4	As the lights crossfade to the downstage cell *Cell door slams, off*	(Page 22)
Cue 5	**Ackroyd**: " ... burdened with religious dogma." *Knock on cell door, off*	(Page 22)
Cue 6	**Jean**: "Let the poor man ——" *Door slams, off*	(Page 38)

ACT II

Cue 7	**Highwood**: " ... law can function as it knows how." *Cell door opens, off*	(Page 39)
Cue 8	Black-out *Cell door closes, off*	(Page 43)
Cue 9	**Jean**: "And now we're strangers." *Knock and cell window sliding open, off*	(Page 48)
Cue 10	**Jean** and **Highwood** fall into each other's arms *Knock on cell door*	(Page 48)